— THE BUDGET —
GARDENING YEAR

Stefan Buczacki

BBC Books

This book is published to accompany the
television series entitled *Bazaar*
which was first broadcast in July 1993

Published by BBC Books,
a division of BBC Enterprises Limited,
Woodlands, 80 Wood Lane
London W12 0TT

First Published 1993
© Dr Stefan Buczacki 1993

ISBN 0 563 36779 2

Designed by Hammond Hammond
Illustrations by Hussein Hussein

Set in Goudy Old Style by
Ace Filmsetting Limited, Frome, Somerset
Printed in Great Britain by Redwood Books, Trowbridge, Wiltshire
Cover printed by Clays Ltd, St Ives Plc

CONTENTS

INTRODUCTION

Many people turn naturally and enthusiastically to gardening as their chosen hobby. Others have it thrust upon them as they realize that their house comes with garden attached and that if they are prepared to give it some care and attention it can enhance both their home and their life. But for all, the pleasure, or potential pleasure, of gardening is bound to be tempered if it begins to make unacceptable inroads into time or money. Gardening really must be enjoyed if it is to be done well and successfully. And, far from costing you money, it should be possible to garden in such a way that it actually saves you expense.

It's obvious from the response that we have had to the gardening items on *Bazaar* that many people agree. They want to garden but they want to garden within a confined budget and they have welcomed the advice we've been able to give. Hence *The Budget Gardening Year*, in which I shall take you through the seasons, highlighting subjects of particular interest at the most appropriate time and giving jobs for each month subdivided into the most important gardening areas. And throughout, I shall give methods and techniques that are economical in both time and money. I start every chapter with my 'Plant of the Month', a cost-effective choice that will offer you the longest possible period of interest and value either side of the time of its peak performance.

The book will work no matter how large or how small your garden but because I am catering for such a wide spectrum, it's obviously not possible for me to set a budget and confine my advice within it. My two over-riding messages, however, are first that you should set your own budget and stick to it. And second, that your guiding principle should be waste not, want not. The very essence of gardening is in recycling – the recycling of organic matter through the compost heap. Extend that philosophy to any number of household items and materials and you will find they can be put to good and virtually cost-free use in the garden. And in the final analysis, whilst any garden success is rewarding, garden success achieved at little or no cost is more rewarding still.

JANUARY

AT THE TURN OF THE YEAR

PLANT OF THE MONTH FOR JANUARY

Erica carnea **'Vivellii' (Winter-flowering heather)**

UNLIKE THE SUMMER flowering heathers which must have acid soils, the winter flowering species, such as *Erica carnea*, will grow almost anywhere and on any type of soil although they are always best in free draining conditions and are least successful on very wet clays. Depending on the variety, they flower on and off between early winter and mid spring and I have selected the rich red variety 'Vivellii' for its superb flower colour which looks particularly appealing when covered with a dusting of snow, its attractive all year round deep greenish bronze foliage and its value as a weed suppressing ground cover. It forms neat growth about 15 cm (6 in) high and a single plant will spread to about 60 × 60 cm (2 × 2 ft) in five years. 'Vivellii' looks especially good when interplanted with the rather more vigorous, white flowered 'Springwood White' in the company of snowdrops and early flowering crocuses.

J	F	M	A	M	J	J	A	S	O	N	D
L	L	L	L	L	L	L	L	L	L	L	L
F	F	F	F							F	F

F flowers, L leaves, Fr fruit, S stems [ ] denotes in some years

PLANNING AHEAD — SOME IDEAS FOR GARDEN DESIGN

I always find the New Year is a period of excitement when we are thinking of the coming season in the garden, but it's also one when the garden can be cold and uninviting. So it provides a fine opportunity for you to do a little planning and see if your garden – be it new or established – really offers you the best. By that I mean the best in terms of an attractive appearance combined with being run on money and labour saving lines.

I don't think many gardeners would disagree that most people's gardens look as they do more by accident than design. They evolve piecemeal as one gardener inherits the layout that the previous owners left, they in turn generally having changed little unless forced to do so – by the lawnmower for ever hitting a misplaced gatepost perhaps, or a wheelbarrow creating ruts that eventually necessitated changing a stretch of lawn into a path. But whether your garden is quite new or already established, there is a great deal to be said for at least some proper planning. A decently thought through plan for your garden will help you to use your time and labour more efficiently and can also help you to create a pleasing effect that makes the most of the size and shape of your plot. Planning is really no more than commonsense and will in itself cost you nothing. And you can plan at two levels – to create something instantly attractive and also a longer term scheme which you can upgrade when your budget allows.

You really need to live with a garden for at least a year before deciding on the majority of changes (and, in an established garden, to see which plants emerge through the spring and summer). Winter, however, does give you time to think carefully about the best ways to proceed.

First, give some thought to exactly what you expect from your garden and to the time that you will have available. Draw up a checklist of questions to be answered:

● **Do you want the garden to be purely ornamental or do you hope to grow at least some edible produce?** If you do want fruit and vegetables, then these must have the sunniest place, consistent with not spoiling your main view. But if your garden is too small to create any suitably hidden areas for fruit and vegetables, then why not integrate them with flowers and shrubs to soften their impact – rows of lettuces or carrots alternating with bedding plants can look most attractive.

● **How much time will you have available?** If your gardening opportunities are really very limited, or you can't get about as much as you'd like, then small plants that need a good deal of watering in the summer don't make much sense – bedding plants and many vegetables come into this category. Confine your summer bedding plants to a few easily watered containers and restrict your choice to those that are most drought-tolerant – pelargoniums and other South African types are good bets.

● **Will much of the time spent gardening be wasted by having to walk from one part to another?** If so, planning your garden to cut down on this will be particularly beneficial. Don't position far from the house those areas that you need to visit most frequently. The vegetable and fruit gardens should be as close as other considerations allow; the herb garden must be close to the kitchen door, as should any flowers being grown specifically for cutting. The compost bin or heap will usually be placed at some fairly far flung corner but do have a trug or other container close at hand to accumulate kitchen and other debris so that one or two visits a week to the compost bin itself are all that is needed.

● **Does your lawn have numerous twists and turns and narrow strips that are barely of mower width?** Are you likely to spend much time negotiating them? If so, redesign the shape of the lawn and widen the strips. Lawn edging is time consuming too, so minimize the number of island beds within a lawn to lessen the work involved here.

● **Which special garden features might you want now or in the future – a greenhouse, a pool, a patio for instance?** All of these need some thought because, like fruit and vegetables, they require a sunny position. As you can see already, the demands on the sunny areas are high and for this reason, it's worth making sure that your shaded places are planted up most efficiently too. I shall have more to say about this later on.

● **Wouldn't you like your garden to be a real delight to your eye and to be admired by your visitors?** Much of the aesthetic appeal of a garden and in fact the success of good garden design comes from making your garden seem larger than it really is. The principle is to give the impression that there are a great many plants whilst you have actually filled rather little of the total area with them. Keep the centre of the garden open and uncluttered with a lawn and site most of the plants around the edge. Use trees or shrubs to obscure the fence or other boundary so it isn't possible to see where the garden actually ends. And if there is a park or other open land beyond the boundary, careful planting can make it appear to be an extension of your own garden. A few strategically placed plants, a simple archway created from old logs, or a glimpse around a corner to reveal nothing more sophisticated than an inexpensive container with a few plants that you have raised yourself can also create an impression of space by promising something hidden beyond the parts that are immediately visible.

Once you have decided that some design or re-design is needed, the simplest way to achieve it is to position yourself at the highest vantage point (which for most people will be an upstairs window) with several sheets of paper.

❀ **'BUDGET TIP'** Save money by sketching your ideas on to old computer paper which you can obtain from offices for the trouble of carrying it away.

Sketch in where the sun rises and sets and note any areas of marked shade or sun. Then indicate where each of your garden features will fit in with these basic constraints. As you work at your garden, make notes of where all of your plants are positioned and then transfer the information to a

A large tree casts a great deal of shade which can swamp a small garden.

neat, master plan (another job for a wet winter day). This information will be invaluable if you lose labels and will also help to prevent you from digging up valuable bulbs or dormant perennials in winter.

You won't be able to afford all of your plans and changes at once. Start therefore with those closest to the house and those which will be most immediately appreciated; and also, if possible, those that will take a long time to mature. If your plans suggest, for instance, that a small tree or shrub is needed in a particular spot as a focal point, it makes sense to buy a small one and plant it straight away. If you wait a couple of years, not only will you miss out on the pleasure of seeing it in place, you will also have to pay more to buy a larger plant to make up for the missing years of growth.

There can be a temptation to think that life will be made easier by the removal of existing trees and large shrubs. It may certainly allow more light into a garden but do be sure that you aren't also removing your privacy and, most importantly, any protection from the wind. You will almost always find that an existing, established tree is better incorporated into your design. If the plant itself is not particularly attractive, then grow climbers over it – this will be a great deal cheaper than replacing it with trellis or some other support that will do exactly the same job. But if after all due consideration you do decide that a tree should be taken down, do check first with your local authority that it isn't subject to a Tree Preservation Order or that it doesn't receive the general protection of being in a Conservation Area. And if the tree is large or threatens buildings, you will almost certainly find that the cost of having the job done professionally will be adequately compensated by peace of mind.

LOOKING AFTER YOUR SOIL

If there is one aspect of gardening that is taken for granted more than any other, it must be the soil. Because all gardens have it in one form or another and because more or less all plants grow in it, we tend to forget how fundamentally important it is and that it actually should be looked after. Winter tends to be the time that gardeners charge into the garden, spade in hand and begin to dig their soil willy-nilly, with little idea of why they do it, how it should be done and often with the simple but understandable belief that the operation is actually designed to do little more than keep them warm.

It is also commonly thought that some soils are quite impossible to work yet in practice no soil is so poor that it can't be gardened – the heaviest clay can be improved, as can the lightest, free-draining sand. I don't pretend that a soil as extreme as these can be changed overnight but with time and effort, and a little cost, they will all come good. Money spent on soil improvement is always money well spent for it will repay you in the long term in better plants and crops.

The improvement of a very heavy or a very light soil isn't a task to be done quickly, however. There is a moral for the gardener who doesn't have a great deal of time and money to spare, which is to concentrate your efforts into a relatively small area (or at least to work through one small bed at a time) and to lay lawn over the remainder (see p. 47 for the relative merits of seed and turf). Soil improvement is not a subject on which to spread your resources and your time thinly.

PRIORITY EXPENDITURE IN THE GARDEN To understand just how soil is best looked after it is well to remember that all soil is made up of mineral particles (either masses of large ones in a sand or masses of minute ones in a clay), together with organic matter or humus. Realistically, you can't change the amounts of mineral particles in the soil but you can do a great deal about enhancing the organic matter which contains natural glues that bind the particles together to form crumbs while leaving gaps between them for aeration and drainage. Every year every soil should have organic matter added and wherever else you economize, I do believe that organic matter should be a priority expenditure. It doesn't matter very much what form the organic matter takes – compost, farmyard or stable manure, leaf mould, mushroom compost; all are valuable and none should be wasted (see Compost Making p. 87). Gardeners who live in fairly rural areas should find little difficulty in obtaining any of these. You will generally find it much cheaper to buy in bulk by the trailer load rather than buying the odd bag or two at the roadside. My experience has been also that road-side bags very often contain mostly straw with a little manure on top – if you can lift them very easily into the boot of your car, be suspicious. Those of you who live in towns or inner cities may need to resort to some proprietary, bagged manures or composts. If you are in this position, choose carefully and buy those that also have some fertilizer added as this will save on your plant feeding bill (see p. 45). For whilst straightforward

Left: dig a trench across the plot, one spade deep and put the soil to one side. *Right:* fork manure or compost in the bottom to the depth of a further spade.

Left: dig a second trench, using the soil to refill the first. *Right:* fork manure into the second trench and gradually work down your plot with more trenches. Finally, refill the last trench with the soil from the first.

JANUARY

organic matter has some plant food content, its main value really is in improving the soil so fertilizer is therefore invariably needed too.

❀ **'BUDGET TIP'** Save money by sharing a trailer load of organic matter with your neighbours.

SOIL STRUCTURE From the importance that I attach to aeration and drainage, you will realize why I say that the crumb and pore structure of the soil should be protected. This might sound an odd notion, but you can best protect the soil's structure by not walking on it. By our constant trampling between rows of vegetables and in and among beds and borders, we flatten the soil, squashing all pores from it and in the process, impeding drainage, preventing nutrients from passing downwards and physically making life extremely hard for the poor little roots that have to try and force a way through. And once soil is compacted in this way, the only remedy is thorough and labour intensive digging.

With ornamental plant beds and shrubberies, try to do as much as possible of your hoeing, spraying and other routine tasks with long-handled tools from the sides. Use a mulch too (see p. 87) which will help lessen the weed growth (and so in turn reduce the amount of work you need to do), and also minimize the hard beating and flattening of the soil surface that can be caused by heavy rain.

In vegetable gardens much the best and easiest way to improve yields and so save money – for it costs nothing – is to adopt the deep-bed method (see p. 59) in which relatively narrow beds are used and in which all parts can be reached easily from the sides. Even this technique of course doesn't eliminate digging altogether but it should restrict it to about once in five years. But when the digging *is* done it should be deep and thorough – double digging. Whereas single digging is digging to the depth of one spade (or one spit as gardeners call it), turning the soil over as you do so, double digging entails digging down to two spade's depth, creating a series of trenches one by one across the bed. Organic matter is forked into the base of each trench and also forked in as the soil from the next trench is used to fill the preceding one. Never try to hurry double digging; it is a job worth doing well and should not need repeating for some considerable time.

JOBS FOR JANUARY

GENERAL

Do winter digging whenever the weather is mild enough; but don't try to dig frozen soil.

Don't forget to feed the birds. They are a gardener's very best friends and I like to think that your kindness now will be repaid in all of the caterpillars that they will eat later in the year.

In mild spells, you may come across a hedgehog awoken from hibernation. They too are valuable in consuming pests, but don't prevent them from being able to do so by misguidedly giving them milk which they are unable to digest.

THE INDOOR GARDEN

Give a little liquid feed every fortnight to flowering house plants

❀ **'BUDGET TIP'** Feed hyacinths until the foliage begins to turn yellow – they are too valuable to throw away and can be planted later in the garden.

Do not water cacti and other succulents and only give water very sparingly to foliage plants.

CONTAINERS

If you haven't already done so, slip small pebbles beneath pots and other containers to raise them and so prolong their life by preventing the damage that can occur if they freeze to the surface on which they are standing.

GREENHOUSES, COLD FRAMES AND CLOCHES

On mild days, open the greenhouse and cold frame to allow ventilation and prevent the build-up of mould which will shorten the productive life of your crops – but be sure to close them again in the evening.

If you have cuttings overwintering in the greenhouse, do be sure to keep the compost on the dry side to avoid any likelihood of rotting – it's a shame to lose such valuable plants after all your care in striking them.

❁ **'BUDGET TIP'** Start collecting together containers for sowing seeds indoors in a few weeks time – yoghurt and margarine pots, plastic salad containers; a little ingenuity will turn all manner of things to good use.

Sow sweet pea seeds in order to obtain a good, early display – there is no better value flower for cutting for the house. To obtain the best germination, soak them overnight and then, if they fail to swell, make a tiny nick in the seeds of dark seeded varieties. Use the tip of a very sharp knife and nick the side of the seed opposite the 'eye'. Sow two seeds in each small pot and pull out the weaker if both germinate. Sweet pea seedlings have long roots and the best pots are made from old toilet or kitchen paper tubes, packed together in a tray, though rolled tubes made from several layers of newspaper held together with a paper-clip can be used instead.

LAWN

Take care to keep off the lawn in frosty weather as walking on frozen grass will damage the foliage and leave brown marks that persist until spring.

In milder spells, use a lawn rake or stiff brush to collect twigs and other debris and disperse worm casts.

THE FLOWER GARDEN

Check any rock garden plants and also any evergreen flowers with woolly or hairy foliage as these are very prone to rotting and decay. Carefully pull away any browned or otherwise damaged leaves before the rot spreads.

As soon as snowdrops and crocuses begin to show above the soil surface, dig up a small clump and bring it indoors in a small pot to produce a cheerful display of early blooms for the house – and so save the cost of buying house-plants.

VEGETABLES

As soon as seed potatoes are in the shops, buy a small bag of a good early variety such as 'Sharp's Express'. The smallest quantity that you can buy

JANUARY

JANUARY

is generally a 3 kg (6.6 lb) bag which will contain about 50 potatoes, enough for a 15 m (16 yd) row from which you should obtain at least 30 kg (66 lb) of crop. Keep the tubers in a cool but frost-free, dark place until next month.

❀ **'BUDGET TIP'** If you only have a very small garden, why not share a bag with a friend.

Cover a clump of rhubarb with an old bucket to force a few young, tender sticks for early in the season – just when they are at their most costly in the shops.

FRUIT

Whenever the temperature isn't actually freezing, spray all fruit canes and bushes, and also fruit trees if they are small enough, with a proprietary tar oil spray. This simple and cheap pest control treatment should save you time and expense in applying insecticides during the summer.

TREES AND SHRUBS

Keep an eye out for tiny tell-tale pink blobs on dead twigs – these indicate coral-spot disease. Cut out and destroy affected shoots before the disease spreads to live branches otherwise you stand the risk of losing precious plants.

CLIMBERS

Check ties and support wires and if any are cutting into the bark, carefully pull them away and re-tie them. If you use plastic covered garden wire, this will last for years, so keep the pieces that you take off for re-use.

Prune wisterias by cutting the long 'whippy' shoots back to just above three buds from the base. This is one of the most valuable and spectacular of garden climbers but you will never benefit from the full glory of its flowers without attention to pruning.

THE COLDEST, BLEAKEST TIME

FEBRUARY

PLANT OF THE MONTH FOR FEBRUARY

Sempervivum arachnoideum **(Cobweb Houseleek)**

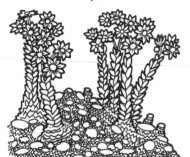

ANYONE WHO LIVES in the country will know the houseleeks. They are among the very hardiest of all succulent plants and derive their common name from their habit of growing on the tiled roofs of old houses and other buildings. Being succulent evergreens, they have an inevitable year-round appeal and I always find them especially welcome and pretty at this cold and cheerless time of the year. Individually most are about 5 cm (2 in) in diameter but they spread to form colonies many times this size. There are many species and varieties and I have chosen the one with a cobweb-like covering, but there are several others that you could select instead. Many change to a reddish green as autumn approaches and from time to time, one or other of the rosettes will thrust forth a spike 15 cm (6 in) of most attractive flowers. The rosette itself then dies to allow its companions to take over. Grow houseleeks in troughs, hollow walls or with your rock plants in well drained gritty soils.

J	F	M	A	M	J	J	A	S	O	N	D
L	L	L	L	L	L	L	L	L	L	L	L
							F	F	F	F	

F flowers, L leaves, Fr fruit, S stems [ ] denotes in some years

PROTECTING YOUR PLANTS

February is the time of the year when the British climate really can be at its most unpleasant and whilst one of the most important features of our weather is that it is not consistently extreme – we don't regularly have very hot summers nor very cold winters – the temperature can fall low enough, especially in the early weeks of the New Year, to cause serious problems for plant life. There is no quicker way to lose money spent on precious

15

FEBRUARY

plants than by allowing them to freeze or chill unnecessarily and it really is very sensible therefore to take precautions before damage can occur.

But the first and most sensible precaution comes from choosing wisely. In general I would always advise gardeners, especially those with small gardens in which gaps soon become obvious, not to put too much faith in plants that are barely hardy in their area. So whilst outdoor fuchsias for example make a good bet in the south of England, they will be unreliable in the north. Even hydrangeas will be at risk in the colder parts of England but they probably fall into the category of plants that can be trusted if you give them some help. In the autumn therefore, mound some compost or other well rotted organic matter around the bases of these marginally hardy plants to protect their crowns from really penetrating frost.

❀ **'BUDGET TIP'** It's a great feature of gardening life that gardeners help each other and so before you spend your money, talk to experienced gardening neighbours who will be happy to advise you if your chosen plant really is hardy enough for your local area.

Evergreens are usually excellent value for the budget gardener, offering instant appeal but they are rather prone to damage from winter cold, particularly when newly planted, so in their first winter, it is worth erecting a temporary screen of old sacking or fairly fine netting around them to keep off the worst of the biting winds.

❀ **'BUDGET TIP'** Old net curtains make a cheap and effective covering.

PROTECTING CONTAINER-GROWN PLANTS Plants in containers are susceptible too as the entire root ball and compost can freeze solid. If possible, move the containers into the most sheltered part of your garden when really hard frost is forecast, but if they are too heavy or nowhere sheltered is available, tie pieces of expanded polystyrene (the type used for packaging) around the pots. Plastic pots are liable to split when their contents freeze and terracotta may crack. If you buy terracotta pots therefore, always obtain the types that are guaranteed to be frost-proof (they will be no more expensive) unless you know that you will be emptying them in autumn for storage somewhere indoors.

WINTER TASKS Although a good deal of gardening activity is curtailed when the weather is very cold, some tasks can certainly continue. No harm will be caused to fruit trees by pruning them in frosty weather (see p. 25) and repairs can be made to fences and other structural garden features (see p. 113) although it is sensible not to lay concrete in freezing conditions. Garden machinery should be checked, cleaned and if necessary serviced during the cold months – and be sure not to leave petrol in powered lawn mowers. You can obtain a simple siphon for emptying the tank from car-care shops. Then leave the top off the tank for a few days to allow any remaining petrol to evaporate. Remember to replace the cap to keep out dust and dirt.

Any garden pool of course will freeze in mid-winter but if it is allowed to do so completely, fish will die from lack of oxygen. I have never found such ideas as floating a rubber ball in the water to keep it ice free are of any use except in the slightest frost. The cheapest and simplest way to thaw the ice is to pour a kettle of boiling water carefully in one corner (but not over the spot where your water-lilies are planted). Never be tempted to take a hammer and smash the ice as the shock waves may well cause severe harm to the fish.

SNOW Snow can cause problems in gardens too and cost you a small fortune. I know all too well, having had many trees and shrubs damaged in a heavy fall a few winters ago. My real difficulty was that I was away from home at the time – the secret is to be on the spot and act quickly and knock off snow from the branches, especially from evergreens, before it has time to build up and freeze solid. If you are away from home when snow threatens, ask a neighbour if he or she would be willing to oblige.

In the open garden, however, snow can actually be beneficial, forming a free of charge protective blanket, rather like a mulch, to prevent the penetration of really hard frost. On greenhouses and cold frames too, I prefer to leave snow on the roof for the same reason – it saves on any heating costs by helping to insulate the structure and protects the plants inside.

USING AND MAKING SIMPLE COLD FRAMES AND CLOCHES

Of all gardening appliances, I am sure that the cold frame and the cloche are the most useful and least expensive to buy. Certainly the cold frame is also the easiest to make at next-to-no expense. Yet both are the most misunderstood and under-appreciated of garden aids.

COLD FRAMES The cold frame has several purposes. It provides a half-way, hardening off halt for plants that have been raised in the relative warmth indoors or in the greenhouse before they are planted fully outside in the open garden. And if you don't have a greenhouse, it offers you at least some protection for slightly tender plants that you wish to keep overwinter. It is worth adding however that, no matter how carefully you insulate it, you really can't expect totally to keep out frost from a cold

FEBRUARY

frame (it isn't called cold for nothing) and so pelargoniums, fuchsias and similarly tender types will still be at risk. In the summer, a cold frame offers an excellent way to grow cucumbers, melons, even miniature tomatoes with the certainty of ripening a crop, even in fairly cold northerly areas.

Most proprietary cold frames are lightweight aluminium structures with glass tops and sides. They are often relatively costly and I find them too flimsy to withstand strong winter winds while their glass sides offer inadequate insulation. Much better is a home-made frame with wooden sides and a top constructed from an old glazed wooden window frame. The length and width dimensions will of course be dictated by the size of window frame you can obtain, but the height of the box structure on which this is placed should be at least 30 cm (12 in) at the front and about 45 cm (18 in) at the back to accommodate the taller types of bedding plant. A slope is essential for rain to run off. The lid can be either loose fitting (although with some form of securing clips) or hinged at the back – but it must provide ventilation in warm weather as this is essential to the correct functioning of a cold frame.

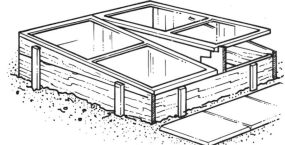

A useful cold frame which can be home-made using an old wooden window frame.

❦ **'BUDGET TIP'** A cold frame will cost you next to nothing if you get discarded timber, bricks and window frames from a local builder.

One difficulty often encountered with cold frames is that worms and slugs are attracted by the warmth and plants inside. Both can be discouraged by using a layer of about 5 cm of crushed cinders, placed over the soil to provide the floor of the frame. Gravel is a second best alternative.

CLOCHES Cloche is a French word for bell and in olden times, the cloche was indeed a bell-shaped and very beautiful object made from glass. Today, these have been replaced with more functional structures but their purpose remains the same – to extend the growing season at the beginning and end (or even overwinter) by providing added warmth in much the same manner as a miniature greenhouse. But unlike a cold frame, the cloche is a movable object and can be placed over plants growing in beds in the kitchen garden. It can also be used, in advance of planting, to warm up the soil to ensure that seedlings and young plants become better established. A couple of weeks of pre-warming can make a great deal of difference to your success rate.

Easily the best and cheapest way to make cloches for individual plants is to cut off the top of old plastic soft drink bottles. You will then be left with something not so different from a traditional old bell cloche which will have the additional advantage of providing free protection from slugs, snails and other predators. Larger cloches, which comprise a transparent tunnel with enclosed ends, are not easy to make from scratch but simple plastic types are inexpensive. The most practical, and yet reasonably robust, for a small area is formed from a tunnel-shaped piece of corrugated clear plastic, anchored with wire hoops over the top and with flat pieces of plastic at either end. Even cheaper but rather more flimsy, although useful for long rows of plants, are the cloches that comprise a series of wire hoops over which a strip of clear plastic sheet is stretched to provide a tunnel, drawn to a knot or clip at each end.

❀ **'BUDGET TIP'** Contact your local glass
merchant for offcuts suitable for cloches.

If you have sheets of waste glass (preferably about 30 × 60 cm [1 × 2 ft] in size), you will find Rumsey clips particularly useful objects. These are inexpensive small 'V'-shaped aluminium clips which hold together two equal-sized sheets of glass to form a simple tunnel of triangular cross-section. You will see Rumsey clips advertised in gardening magazines and they are well worth having because the advantage of glass over plastic is that it retains heat better and for longer.

PLANNING A SMALL GREENHOUSE

You will need to be pretty well above average in the DIY business if you contemplate making your own greenhouse. However, the cost of small greenhouses has fallen dramatically in recent years and a very simple lean-to structure (almost a vertical cold frame) can be bought for under £40. Even an unheated structure such as this will enable you to grow more plants and so add a new dimension to your gardening enjoyment. But do spend another pound or two and buy some double film plastic insulation to fit over the inside. The greenhouse manufacturer can supply clips to enable this to be done easily – although at a pinch (I use the word advisedly) you can improvise with clothes pegs.

FEBRUARY

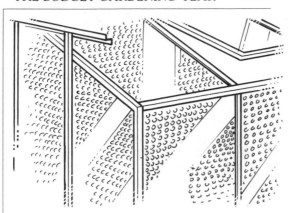

❀ **'BUDGET TIP'** A free source of greenhouse insulation is waste bubble film plastic of the type used for packaging but this will tend to deteriorate rather more quickly than proprietary types of insulation.

Position your greenhouse in the sunniest spot – preferably against a south or south west facing wall. With small greenhouses however, I don't advise painting the wall white to reflect light as is often recommended for lean-tos – it can cause over-heating. But do be sure that your greenhouse has plenty of shelving. A small greenhouse must function essentially like a walk-in cupboard.

❀ **'BUDGET TIP'** Make your own shelving. Old lengths of thin planking can be screwed to the aluminium structure of the greenhouse by anyone reasonably handy to make the shelves.

Uses for an unheated greenhouse

March	April	May	June	July	August	September	October	November	December	January	February
SPRING			SUMMER			AUTUMN			WINTER		
Raise tomato plants											
			Take cuttings								
			Raise house plants from seed								
Move bedding plants to cold frame for hardening off						Raise summer bedding plants and vegetables from seed					
						Store dahlia tubers, gladioli and other fairly robust plants					
									Sprout potato tubers		

FEBRUARY

MAKING THE BEST USE OF THE GREENHOUSE How then will the greenhouse be cost-effective? First by raising as many as possible of your summer bedding plants and vegetables. The cost of bedding plants bought by the tray can soon mount and yet for the price of the seeds and a bag of proprietary compost, you can save pounds and have plants in plenty for yourself and some spare for friends too. Then, as soon as they are large enough to be moved on to the cold frame for hardening off in April, the greenhouse will be ready to accommodate a couple of tomato plants in a growing bag if you remove the shelves from one half. You should also have room for taking cuttings through the summer and into early autumn and for raising house plants from seed. Once autumn does come, the greenhouse, given that all-important insulation, will be protected enough to supply overwintering space for dahlia tubers, gladioli and other fairly robust tubers and bulbs so that they can be used again. And in the New Year, you can use it for sprouting potato tubers before planting. The cost of the greenhouse will thus very soon be recovered in your savings on new plants.

With a small paraffin heater you can be sure that your greenhouse will stay frost free through winter. This will open up a whole new world of overwintering pelargonium and fuchsia cuttings, even growing some of the hardier orchids such as cymbidiums and in fact the many other types of tender plant that will 'tick over' at temperatures just above freezing. Many of them can be raised from seed so you won't even have the cost of initial 'stock' plants. You could save a great deal of money on house plants, therefore, simply by raising your own; and never forget that there will be no such thing as spares because pot plants make the most wonderfully appreciated presents.

❀ **'BUDGET TIP'** Small paraffin heaters are often found at car boot sales or similar events, but do check they work properly and always remember to clean them regularly and to trim the wick.

JOBS FOR FEBRUARY

GENERAL

If you live in a rural area or know someone with hedgerows on their land, ask if you may collect bundles of twigs for use as pea sticks or supports for herbaceous plants. In country areas, you may well see farmers doing routine hedging at this time of year and they will generally be more than happy for you to take away a few bundles. They are very effective plant supports and cost nothing; but never cut twigs without the owner's permission.

FEBRUARY

THE INDOOR GARDEN

❀ **'BUDGET TIP'** Think what a wonderfully cheap and appreciated gift a home-grown cyclamen would make, so buy cyclamen seeds to produce flowering pot plants for next winter. Sow them in small pots of compost, germinate them in the airing cupboard (keep checking, they take some time) and then grow them on on the window ledge.

Plant a few cloves of garlic in a pot on the window ledge. These will soon produce fresh green shoots that will add a splendid tang to your early season salads.

CONTAINERS

As soon as bulbs begin to peep through the soil surface, in both containers and the open garden, scatter a little bone meal around them to give them an early season feed and so help them on their way to a good show of blooms.

GREENHOUSES, COLD FRAMES AND CLOCHES

Pelargoniums, aubergines and peppers are the plants that require the longest growing season. If you sow them now in an airing cupboard they will germinate quickly and can then be moved first to the window ledge and then to the greenhouse (if it is frost-free).

❀ **'BUDGET TIP'** When buying pelargonium seed, choose the F_2 rather than the F_1 hybrid varieties – you will have mixtures rather than single colours but the seeds are very much cheaper.

LAWN

If the weather is mild, it isn't too soon to give the lawn a very light mowing – but only do this if you have a rotary type of mower and even then, if the cutters are adjustable, set them to their highest level. Cylinder mowers cut too close for this early in the season.

THE FLOWER GARDEN

Check over your winter bedding plants – pansies, wallflowers and primulas – and pull away any damaged leaves. This will prolong their lives for weeks and ensure that they give you the very best value.

VEGETABLES

Set out your 'seed' potato tubers on end with the cluster of 'eyes' uppermost on trays, in a light, fairly warm place so they sprout.

FEBRUARY

Dig a few roots of mint and place them shallowly in compost in a small pot on the window ledge. Keep the compost damp and you will soon have delicious green shoots to use with the new season's lamb at a time when fresh herbs are so expensive in the shops.

As soon as the soil is fairly dry, plant a few cloves of garlic. Buy a single bulb from the greengrocer or supermarket and split it up for planting outside. Set each clove about 20 cm (8 in) apart just pushed in below the surface; preferably place a cloche over the top. By late summer you will have masses to keep for next winter.

FRUIT

Prune autumn-fruiting raspberries such as the very good, new variety 'Autumn Bliss' by cutting all canes back to soil level.

Prune apple and pear trees – young trees should be pruned as I have shown on p. 26. Old trees generally require little more than cutting out damaged, diseased or crossing branches.

TREES AND SHRUBS

Prune 'butterfly bush' buddleias by cutting all shoots back to about 25 cm (10 in) above soil level. It may seem very drastic but it's essential to keep the plant in good shape.

If a hollow has formed in the soil around the bases of trees and shrubs, be sure to refill and firm it – otherwise it will trap water, causing rotting and so bring about the loss of valuable plants.

CLIMBERS

Prune clematis as soon as you have a few mild days (see p. 26).

THE GARDEN STIRS INTO LIFE

PLANT OF THE MONTH FOR MARCH

Viola tricolor **(Wild pansy)**

IT WILL PERHAPS take a fairly mild March to see the wild pansy in flower but I have recorded it blooming in my own garden in every month of the year. It might seem odd to choose an annual for year-round interest but I make no apology, partly because *Viola tricolor* can be a short-lived perennial but also because it self-seeds with such profusion that you never know just how long any particular plant has been growing and so consequently it is good value for money. It has the characteristic pansy 'face' on tiny, perfectly formed flowers and will reach about 28 cm (11 in) in height. You can sow it once and it will be with you forever. And sow it almost anywhere you wish. If self seeds all over my kitchen garden and to keep it within bounds, I merely have to weed out the plants that are growing where it is least convenient. The remainder make a wonderful display against the lush green of my vegetables and salads.

J	F	M	A	M	J	J	A	S	O	N	D
[F]	[F]	F	F	F	F	F	F	F	F	F	F

F flowers, L leaves, Fr fruit, S stems [ ] denotes in some years

PRUNING

Nothing will improve your plants more, at absolutely no cost and for so little effort, than pruning and for some of the most important garden plants (roses especially), the pruning season is in early spring. If you remember a few basic facts about pruning, you will never go far wrong.

● Pruning improves the shape and/or the flowering of a plant by removing unattractive or worn out parts in order to give new buds the opportunity to burst.

MARCH

- It allows light and air into the centre of the plant.
- It also eliminates the possibility of diseases gaining a foothold.
- By cutting out dead, damaged, crossing or diseased parts of a plant, be they branches on a tree or flower heads on an annual, you will improve its performance and so induce it to give the best return for your money.

PRUNING ORNAMENTAL SHRUBS AND CLIMBERS The pruning of ornamental shrubs and climbers is much more logical when the reason for its timing is understood. Always prune *after* they have flowered and you will not cut away the current season's blooms.

In practice, those types that flower before midsummer should be pruned immediately after flowering and generally rather lightly – not much more than tidying up. Those that flower *after* midsummer may be pruned immediately but, if they are slightly tender, are better left until early in the following spring. And most of these later flowering types need rather harder pruning. In every case, always make your pruning cut just above a bud.

There are a few important and special categories that often cause concern: roses, fruit, clematis and wisterias.

PRUNING ROSES For simplicity, prune all roses in March:
- hybrid teas – cut back all of their shoots by about half;
- floribundas – cut back the oldest third of the shoots nearly to the base and the remainder by about one-third of their length;
- on climbing versions of these types, cut back all the flowered side-shoots to about 5 cm (2 in) above the basic framework.

PRUNING FRUIT BUSHES AND TREES Pruning is especially important in the fruit garden to increase yields. Techniques vary between the types of plant:
- Summer-fruiting raspberries, blackberries, loganberries and similar cane fruits – cut all of the old fruited canes back to soil level immediately after fruiting;
- Autumn fruiting raspberries – cut back *all* canes to soil level in February.
- Blackcurrants – cut out the oldest and lowest third of the shoots in winter and then cut back the remaining shoots by about one-third of their length;
- Gooseberries and red and white currants – cut back all side branches to just above six leaves from their junction with the main branches in late summer, and then cut them again back to 5 cm (2 in) above the junction in winter;
- Fruit trees – follow the diagrams on p. 26.

MARCH

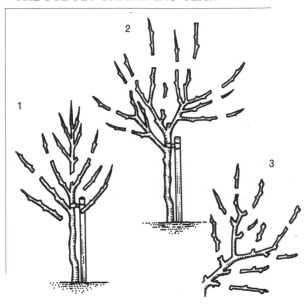

1. In the first winter, cut the main shoot back hard to leave three or four branches only, and cut these back by about one-third.

2. In the next winter, cut back the side-shoots by about one-third.

3. In future winters, cut back the side-shoots by about one-quarter – the aim is to have to cut off less and less each year.

PRUNING CLEMATIS AND WISTERIA Clematis pruning actually follows my general rules but, for greatest effect and simplicity, remember the following:
● Early spring flowering types should be pruned immediately after flowering with a light tidying up;
● Summer flowering types should be pruned in February by cutting out up to one third of last season's growth;
● Late summer- and autumn-flowering types should be pruned in February by cutting them back to about 75 cm (30 in) above soil level.

Wisterias should be pruned first in summer by cutting back all of the long, whippy shoots to about 25 cm (10 in) above their base, and then again in winter by cutting them back again to about 5 cm (2 in) above the base.

SOWING SEEDS INDOORS

Raising your own plants from seed absolutely epitomizes cost-saving gardening and the month of March is always a busy one for gardeners who raise their own plants indoors. By sowing any seeds indoors (either inside the house or in a greenhouse) you will give them a head start over those sown directly in the garden. This means a longer growing season and greater productivity. Some types in fact must be sown indoors because they require higher temperatures to grow, cannot tolerate frost and would never have long enough in a British summer to produce anything worthwhile if they had to spend their entire life in the garden. The flowers and those very few vegetables such as tomatoes that *must* be started in warmth are called half-hardy annuals. Those that can be sown outdoors are called hardy annuals.

❀ **'BUDGET TIP'** You might be able to save money by using seed saved from the previous year. Test sow a few seeds indoors first of both hardy and half-hardy varieties. If you obtain good germination, then use the bulk of the seeds but, if your test sowing produces little, you will need a fresh packet.

SOWING IN A CONTAINER To sow seeds indoors, you need two basic items: first, some sowing compost and second, some form of seed tray or similar container. Using garden soil is not a good idea because it may contain pests and diseases and will almost certainly become heavy, impenetrable and glue-like once it is placed in a seed tray and watered. And your seeds will be wasted. A small 5 kg (11 lb) bag of proprietary sowing compost will fill several seed trays for under £2. Try if possible to choose one of the new, peat-free composts such as coconut coir. Reusable plastic seed trays cost under £1 each, although you can use almost any small plastic container provided you make some provision for drainage.

❀ **'BUDGET TIP'** Save money by combining a food-shopping trip with stocking up on your garden needs. Some supermarkets sell salads, cakes and chocolates in shallow plastic trays that are excellent for seed raising. And of course, if you want only half a dozen plants of any particular type, then plastic drinking cups and yoghurt pots (make a few drainage holes in the base with a hot knitting needle) are ideal.

❀ **'BUDGET TIP'** A child's watering can is often cheaper than a specialized one for indoor plants and is ideal for watering container-grown plants.

The compost should be gently pressed into the tray, watered carefully and the seeds sown as described on the packet – some types should be scattered, others sown in drills (shallow grooves). Some seeds should be covered with compost and others left uncovered. But don't sow too many seeds – even if you sow twice as many as you will need plants, this will still leave room for several different types of seed in each tray, provided each is labelled. And do read your seed packets carefully – they are the best source of free gardening information that I know.

❀ **'BUDGET TIP'** Cheap labels can be obtained by cutting up any white plastic food container and writing on it with a clothes marking pen.

The seed tray will need a cover to retain moisture until the seeds have germinated. The simplest way to achieve this is with a plastic bag, slipped over the top, supported at each of the four corners (old ballpoint pens are ideal) and secured with a rubber band. Some seeds require

MARCH

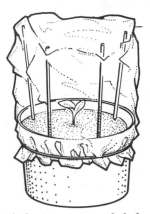

much higher temperatures than others to germinate – and some such as cyclamen and primroses take very much longer. If your seed packet tells you that a temperature of 18°C (64°F) or above is required, place the tray complete with its cover in the airing cupboard. But do keep a close eye on it and remove it to somewhere light such as a warm window ledge as soon as the first signs of green shoots appear. Prick out a few seedlings at a time as their first true leaves appear (see p. 36).

You will almost certainly have some seeds left over in the packet but whatever you do, don't throw them away. You can save pounds simply by storing them carefully. Most types of seed will keep for at least two years and some for even longer (peas and beans and similar very large seeds are the most unreliable). The enemies of seeds are warmth and damp so place the closed packets in a screw-top jar and keep this in the bottom of the fridge.

❀ **'BUDGET TIP'** If by chance you have a sachet of silica gel (these are often packed with new electrical goods) pop this in the seed jar too; it will absorb some of the moisture and help keep the seeds fresh.

You should do exactly the same with seeds that you save from your own plants (see p. 80).

CHOOSING AND USING CLIMBERS

One of the delights of my garden in spring lies in the appearance of the early flowering clematis, followed by wisteria and then my climbing roses. I can't imagine how bare my garden would look without its many attractive climbing plants. And not only do climbers look colourful, they also make more of your space; in small gardens especially, leaving all of the vertical surfaces unclothed is so much wasted growing area. Some of the most attractive climbers (clematis especially) are very inexpensive.

Not all climbers are suitable for all situations. The more vigorous types such as *Clematis montana*, honeysuckle or some climbing roses are much better if they can be allowed free rein. This really means that they aren't appropriate in very small gardens, which are unlikely to contain a tree large and robust enough to support them. In limited space, choose

MARCH

a less vigorous clematis such as the large flowered hybrid 'The President', white summer jasmine or the more restrained climbing roses – especially those commonly called pillar roses which look delightful when grown up a single post. An old tree trunk looks wonderful when adorned in this way and if you don't have one in situ, have a word with a local tree surgeon; they are usually more than glad to find a home for old logs.

<u>TYPES OF CLIMBER</u> It is important to distinguish between those climbers such as clematis with tendrils that are more or less able to tie themselves on to their trellis and those such as roses which must be tied with loose wire or string – and I stress 'loose' because eventually a tight wire will cut into and harm the stems. There is in fact a third category of so-called self-clinging climbers such as the ivies and some of the Virginia creeper types of vine. These have adhesive aerial roots that attach to vertical surfaces such as brickwork. Most are fairly vigorous and can damage crumbly bricks and mortar. They are perfectly safe on sound brick or stone however and are a cheap way to cover unsightly buildings.

<u>CARING FOR CLIMBERS</u> There are two main ways that you can provide support for climbers: either they can be allowed to grow as they do naturally, scrambling over other plants such as large trees; or you can provide artificial support, such as trellis or a house wall. On house walls, you will need a few strips of wooden batten to raise the plants from the surface but to erect specially made trellis can be very pricey.

❀ **'BUDGET TIP'** For better value and greater durability choose plastic so-called clematis net rather than the diamond patterned and rather flimsy wooden type.

Most common climbing plants are easy to grow but do bear in mind that the soil close to a wall or fence is likely to be rather dry. It is important

Here clematis has been trained on trellis which has been fastened to a wall.

therefore to pay extra attention to watering in dry spells and also to be sure that the plants have the soil around them covered with a moisture retaining mulch of compost in spring. You may also find that mildew and aphids tend to be a little more severe close to a wall (see p. 67).

BEDDING PLANTS

Bedding plants are annuals that are used widely to provide colour through the summer, either edging beds and borders or in window boxes and other containers. Among the best known are lobelia, marigolds, petunias, asters and impatiens (Busy Lizzies). There is no denying that bedding plants are appealing but they can represent a rather expensive way of colouring your garden. Most of the best are half-hardy or at least need a good boost to their early growth and so they must be raised indoors with warmth. Warmth is expensive and if you buy them from the garden centre or DIY store, you must expect to pay £2–3 per tray or half-tray.

My advice therefore is two-fold. First, think very carefully how many plants you really need. There's no point putting them where they won't be very obvious so save money by restricting your planting to containers and to small beds very close to the house. And be especially careful in buying pelargoniums which are the most costly of all. The odd plant as a centre piece can be as effective as a whole mass. And second, ask yourself if you couldn't raise at least some of the plants at home. However you obtain your plants, do be sure to water them regularly and feed at least once a week with liquid fertilizer, and snip off the dead flower heads promptly.

JOBS FOR MARCH

GENERAL

As you empty your seed packets why not paste them into a scrap book for future reference? They contain masses of useful information and it is such a shame to throw it all away.

THE INDOOR GARDEN

As the days lengthen begin to give a little water and liquid feed to cacti and other succulents – water once a fortnight and feed every three weeks.

Dead head spring flowering house plants regularly.

Indoor plants that have been in the same pot for more than three years will probably be in need of re-potting and this should be done around the middle of the month. Choose a pot about one size larger than the current one, knock the plant from its old pot, gently tease the roots slightly from around the sides of the root-ball and then pack new compost around it in its new pot. Finally, it should be given a thorough watering.

CONTAINERS

If you have lilies in containers (much the best way to grow them), they will benefit from a mulch of compost or, best of all, leaf mould mixed with a scattering of bonemeal as the new shoots emerge.

If you need more containers for your summer bedding plants, now is the time to keep an eye open for likely materials.

❀ **'BUDGET TIP'** Old buckets, sinks, paint cans, car tyres, all can be turned into cheap containers with a good clean, a coat of paint and some drainage holes.

❀ **'BUDGET TIP'** As good compost is a necessity, it makes sense to buy a small bag as and when you can afford it rather than suddenly finding at the end of May that you need half a dozen.

Large tubs can be prepared by simply replacing the top few centimetres of compost and raking in a little general fertilizer.

GREENHOUSES, COLD FRAMES AND CLOCHES

Multiply your stock of half hardy perennials such as pelargoniums, dahlias and fuchsias by taking soft wood cuttings now (see p. 70). They will need to be hardened off in due course in the same way as seed-raised plants but you will be able to multiply a single overwintered stock plant up to ten or more times. Dahlias needed for cuttings should be planted shallowly in fairly dry, old, soil-less compost around the beginning of March but those that are to be planted directly outside as tubers should be kept in their winter wrapping until April.

Most types of half hardy bedding plants may now be sown anywhere indoors that you have warm space. Do remember, however, that the young plants will need pricking on and hardening off and will then take up a great deal more frost-free space. So only sow as many as you really do have room for.

Tomatoes may be sown this month for planting out in six weeks time. If you will be growing them outdoors, this can be done only at the end of May and so the middle of March will be soon enough to sow. If you possess a greenhouse, a porch, or somewhere else sheltered, then you will be able to sow a good two weeks earlier than this.

❀ **'BUDGET TIP'** Choose the variety 'Gardener's Delight' for the very best, sweetest-flavoured but small fruits. If you prefer a larger-fruited variety, then follow my advice and grow 'Alicante' which over many years I have found the most reliable. Both may be grown indoors or out.

MARCH

Even this early in the season, the greenhouse can become very warm so open ventilators around the middle of the day but close them at night and apply a shade paint (from garden centres) to the outside. Unfortunately, you can't make do with white-wash or emulsion paint instead as these either wash off with rain or become completely irremovable.

LAWN

Rake or brush the lawn and continue mowing occasionally too if conditions allow. If there are bare patches to be renewed or if you plan to sow or turf a new lawn, now is the time to prepare the soil by digging and fertilizing. But don't give the soil of your prospective new lawn its final raking yet – wait until just before you are ready to start next month for otherwise the soil will form an impervious 'cap' after heavy rain.

THE FLOWER GARDEN

Make the first sowings of hardy annual flowers such as candytuft and alyssum in soil raked and prepared with a little general fertilizer.

Continue to dead-head winter bedding plants and they will produce extra flowers as the temperatures rise.

As the flowers fade on snowdrops and aconites, they can be lifted, moved and the clumps divided to give you many more plants. These two are among the few types of bulbs best moved when in full leaf.

Dead head all spring flowering bulbs and give them liquid feed every fortnight for six weeks, after which the foliage may be cut back.

As soon as the first shoots emerge on herbaceous perennials, give them a small handful of general fertilizer. And put supports in place as soon as possible – you will damage the stems if you leave it too late.

Sweet peas sown in late January should have their tips pinched out as soon as they have four true leaves (usually around the beginning of the month). They will then be ready for planting out at the end of the month. Dig a circular patch of soil and fork in as much compost as possible. then erect a wigwam of canes or sticks around the area and place a single plant at the foot of each cane. Sweet peas may need tying in initially but will soon climb of their own accord.

VEGETABLES

By March the first seeds of hardy outdoor varieties can be sown in well prepared soil. For the most cost-effective results be sure to use varieties classed as 'early'.

Sow a small patch of parsley, provided the soil isn't waterlogged; it is slow to germinate and so the sooner you make a start the sooner you will be able to savour the unmatched taste of fresh green sprigs.

By the end of the month, in almost all areas, the early potatoes may be planted. Place the tubers, sprouts uppermost, about 10 cm (4 in) deep and 30 cm (12 in) apart. Draw soil over them when the shoots emerge above the soil to protect them from frost damage.

FRUIT

By the end of March, you should have completed planting any bare-rooted trees and bushes that were not put in in autumn. Although you will be able to plant out container-grown plants right through summer, the sooner this is done and the plants are established, the more likely will you be to obtain a good crop in the first year.

Put a compost mulch around young fruit trees and bushes to help retain moisture in the soil and save work in watering later. Also give all young plants a handful of a general fertilizer.

Peach trees are almost the only fruit trees that can be grown reliably from seed. Plant a stone now in a pot of compost and you will not only have an attractive ornamental tree for nothing but also, in a few years time, you should have your own crop.

For anyone with an established peach tree, remember to help pollination by dusting the flowers now with a light paint brush – there aren't many bees about at this time of year.

TREES AND SHRUBS

All types of roses should be pruned before the month is out. And immediately after pruning give them a handful of general fertilizer to ensure that they reward you with a good crop of early season blooms.

Early flowering shrubs such as winter jasmine, winter-flowering heathers and forsythia may be pruned lightly by cutting back the old flowered shoots as soon as their blooms have faded.

The dead shoots left on over winter to give protection to slightly tender shrubs such as 'hardy' fuchsias and hydrangeas may now be cut off.

CLIMBERS

Start to prune foliage climbers such as ivies and parthenocissus as soon as the weather becomes a little milder. On very large climbers you can use shears but, ideally, a pair of secateurs is the best tool and will give the neatest effect with least damage to the foliage.

WET, WINDY AND VERY BUSY

PLANT OF THE MONTH FOR APRIL

Amelanchier lamarckii (Juneberry, Serviceberry, Shadberry Snowy Mespil)

IT REALLY IS rather difficult to choose the best month to feature this magnificent little tree for it truly seems to have something to offer for the whole year. In spring, it is covered with masses of tiny white flowers at the same time as the leaf buds unfold with coppery green splendour. Right through the summer it is bedecked with small, delicate leaves until these turn a rich and lovely orange in autumn. If you are lucky and the birds leave them alone, there may be a crop of tiny black berries. Even when leafless in the winter, the branches have a delicate tracery that few other deciduous trees can match. And if this wasn't commendation enough, the plant is trouble-free: it suffers from no ailments, needs no pruning, will grow in almost any soil, including heavy clay, and is tolerant of strong winds. It really is the answer to a budget gardener's prayer.

J	F	M	A	M	J	J	A	S	O	N	D
					FR	FR	FR	FR			
S	S	S	F	L	L	L	L	L	L	L	S

F flowers, L leaves, Fr fruit, S stems [ ] denotes in some years

SOWING SEEDS OUTDOORS

Sowing seeds yourself outdoors in the garden, with soil, sunshine, rain and fresh air as the main stimulants for growth really is the essence of cost-saving gardening. And as the soil in the garden begins to warm up in April, seed sowing outdoors can begin in earnest. A good tip that indicates when nature is ready, is to note when weed seedlings begin to appear in quantity. But do remember that half-hardy plants and among vegetables, this applies most importantly to runner beans, cucumbers and courgettes,

APRIL

should not be sown until about two weeks before the danger of the last frost has passed (see p. 55). For most parts of the country, it will be safe to sow half-hardy plants by mid-May.

Success will be pretty well guaranteed if you use good seed and take care to prepare the soil. It must be lightly dug over and all weeds removed and then raked carefully to take off large stones and clods – seedlings can't grow through lumpy soil. Do the final raking about one week before you are ready to sow and as you do so, gently scatter a little fertilizer (fish, blood and bone is an excellent organic mix) over the surface. You will obtain the best germination if the soil is pre-warmed before you sow. This can be done most satisfactorily with cloches (see p. 17) but, failing these, simply anchoring plastic sheet over the soil will help. The advantage of cloches over plastic sheet, however, is that the former can be replaced over the newly sown seeds to keep them warm; the sheet would prevent the seedlings from emerging.

❋ **'BUDGET TIP'** If a packet contains too many seeds for your requirements, why not save money and please a friend by sharing the packet with him or her? Or, sow the entire seed packet yourself and swop the surplus seedlings with theirs of a different type.

HOW TO SOW There is still a good deal of mystery attached to seed sowing. Although sowing depths and spacings between seeds and between rows vary for different types of plant (you will find details on the packets), the actual groove or drill into which the seeds are placed is similar for most types. Use the back of a rake, or simply a bamboo cane, to make a drill approximately 5–10 mm (¼–½ in) deep. After sowing the seeds, carefully draw the soil back over them and then gently press it down. This is the key to success – press too hard or leave the soil too loose and emergence will be less than ideal. When sowing annual flowers as opposed to vegetables it is generally more satisfactory to rake a shallow patch and sow the seeds in a small group rather than in separate rows.

Carefully pull out any weeds that emerge between the seedlings and pay attention to guidance on the packet about thinning. Almost invariably, more seedlings will grow than can properly mature and you must pull out the excess to leave the correct spacings. Overcrowded seedlings will become diseased and be a waste of money. But don't waste the extras; with many types of plant, the thinnings can be used to fill in gaps or planted elsewhere in the garden, but be sure not to let their roots dry out.

APRIL

TRANSPLANTING

Seedlings raised indoors must be transplanted into the open garden as soon as they are large enough to be handled safely. For most types, this will be between four and six weeks after sowing. And sometimes young plants raised in one spot outdoors must be moved to another. But seedlings from indoors, whether they are hardy or half-hardy must first be hardened off – that is, gradually accustomed to the somewhat cooler conditions outside. The ideal way to do this is with a cold frame (see p. 17). I do hardening off in the cold frame on a two-week cycle. In the first week, the lid is half open in the daytime and closed at night. In the second week, it is fully open in the daytime and half closed at night.

When transplanting, always lift the plants with a generous amount of soil around their roots. Nothing so checks their growth as damage to young and fragile roots. Having taken care and money to raise seedlings this far, it is tragic to lose them now. When replanting, firm the soil around them carefully and then – a personal tip – water them in with liquid fertilizer, not plain water. It will help them re-establish very much more quickly. For details on transplanting large plants see p. 96.

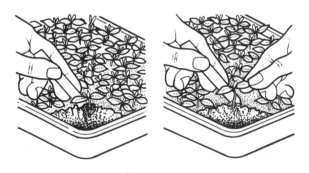

Far left: pricking out seedlings should be done individually. *Left:* hold the seedling by the leaves *not* the roots.

WEEDS AND WEED CONTROL

You will never garden profitably and successfully if you allow weeds to compete with your garden plants – the weeds always win. By the simple expedient of controlling the weeds, you can ensure bigger and better plants at little or no cost. There are three main groups of weed and they need rather different treatment.

ANNUAL WEEDS Annual weeds are the most numerous and also easiest to combat. They come up in droves every year but are kept in check by two techniques, both costing nothing except the labour of doing them. The first is by mulching in autumn or early spring. Spread a thick layer of compost, about 5 cm (2 in) over the soil surface and no weed seedlings will be able to penetrate. In dry weather, and especially among vegetables

where mulching isn't really practicable, adopt the second technique and use a hoe to slice down weed growth. Hoeing in wet weather is of no value because the weeds will simply be moved around.

PERENNIAL WEEDS Perennial weeds such as thistles can usually be dug up and disposed of, but the really deep-rooted species such as bindweed, couch grass, horsetail and ground elder can't realistically be controlled by digging, even on a light soil. The answer lies in a bottle of weedkiller – 'Tumbleweed', 'Greenscape' or 'Roundup' – containing the chemical glyphosate (cost about £2.25). This will be absorbed by the plant and is very effective but must be applied in warm, dry weather; and you will need to repeat the treatment several times. Do remember not to spray other plants because glyphosate is a total weedkiller, although it is inactivated in the soil.

LAWN WEEDS The third main group of weeds comprises those that infest lawns – dandelions, daisies, clover and the rather pretty blue-flowered creeping speedwell are among the commonest. Frustratingly these are the types of weed that can withstand mowing. To some extent, dandelions and daisies can be kept in check by digging them up with a two-pronged daisy grubber tool or even with an old fork. Unfortunately, dandelions and some other species will regenerate from root fragments left behind. And there really is no mechanical method by which to remove the mat-forming weeds, although you can limit their spread to some extent by keeping the grass collector (if you have one) on the mower. Again, the real answer is a weedkiller and there are two ways to apply this. The smallest size of a spring lawn fertilizer (see p. 42) such as 'Toplawn', which has a weedkiller incorporated, costs about £1.80 for 14 sq. m (16.7 sq. yd). This is slightly more than the price of a basic lawn fertilizer for a comparable area. My feeling is that the minimal difference is worth paying even though the chances are that you will still need a top-up weedkiller treatment later in the summer. A 100 ml (3.5 fl. oz) bottle of a specific lawn weedkiller will cost about £1.50 and will treat 50 sq. m (60 sq. yd).

APRIL

YEAR-ROUND COLOUR IN YOUR GARDEN

Far too many gardeners complain to me that their gardens look pretty in the spring when the bulbs are in bloom, go through a dismal period in early summer until the bedding plants paint everything with their bright colours, then turn rather brown again from late July until the flowers and leaves of autumn cheer them up once more, and then finally turn grey when everything shuts up shop for winter. No garden need be like this and there are essentially two ways to achieve colour continuity. The first but most expensive is by having a large number of plants, each in flower for a relatively short period. In a budget garden however this is quite impractical and with fewer plants in total, the effect must be obtained more economically by using the second way. This is to have plants that individually offer some interest for a long period. My top 12 plants to give the best year-round colour appeal are highlighted at the top of each chapter but it is worth outlining the features to look for.

*E*laeagnus pungens 'Maculata' is one of the most valuable and easy of evergreens for winter colour. The vivid yellowish leaf patterns intensify dramatically with the onset of cold weather.

FOLIAGE PLANTS Evergreens will generally provide longer appeal than deciduous types and your best bet will be with those that offer a change in foliage colour, such as the variegated *Elaeagnus pungens* 'Maculata', which increases the intensity of its variegation in winter. Alternatively, try evergreen shrubs such as pyracanthas that also have good flower and berry interest. Among deciduous foliage shrubs, there are several aspects to consider. Visit your garden centre in early spring and see which types are already in leaf – and then discover which drop their leaves late in the autumn (preferably after turning an attractive colour) in order to provide the longest period of interest. An appealing bark colour, such as is found with dogwoods, or attractive winter buds, as on some of the dwarf willows, will also enhance the garden worthiness of deciduous plants.

FLOWERING PLANTS Flowering shrubs that provide the longest period of bloom will of course be the most cost-effective for the budget gardener.

So choose climbing rather than rambling roses, and modern hybrid teas or floribundas rather than old shrub varieties. Potentillas and, among half-hardy types, fuchsias, bloom probably for longer than any other type of flowering shrub. A selection of long-flowering border perennials should include phlox, hardy geraniums and Michaelmas daisies. With bulbs it isn't easy to find individual varieties that bloom for a long period but choose a range of varieties among daffodils and narcissi, tulips and crocuses to give continuity. For the best effect, don't mix the varieties together but keep them in separate clumps. And try to choose those that are fairly small so that you will be able to get the best value for money by including the greatest variety in a small space.

And do visit your garden centre or nursery in winter. But don't restrict yourself to the house plant section. Walk around the outside beds too and just see what is in flower – you will be surprised at the way some of them could enhance your own garden.

ROCK GARDENS AND RAISED BEDS

The plants that are sometimes called rock plants or alpines have a great deal to offer to the gardener with limited funds and space. Although the majority flower in the spring, it is possible to select a range of varieties that between them offer flowers right through the year. And almost all have attractive and varied foliage and growth habits too. As plants they are individually very inexpensive and several types can be grown from seed.

In times gone by these plants were grown in vast rock gardens that were little less than scaled down versions of the Alps. Today much the best way of displaying them is in a trough garden or a raised bed.

An old sink can easily be adapted to make an attractive trough garden.

TROUGH GARDENS Troughs of real stone are impossibly expensive although reproduction ones in a range of attractive designs are really quite reasonably priced. But much the simplest way to obtain a trough is to make one yourself.

APRIL

You will need either an old sink with a drainage hole, or a framework of chicken-wire. A glazed sink will first require a coat of adhesive to provide 'grip'; for the substitute stone, which is a material called hypertufa. This is made by mixing equal parts by volume of sand, cement and sphagnum peat with water to produce the consistency of thick porridge. It should then be pasted on the sink or chicken-wire. It will soon harden and then, by painting lightly with fresh cow manure or milk, algae and lichens will be attracted to grow and complete the illusion of real stone.

❀ **'BUDGET TIP'** Don't cover the drainage hole in the sink otherwise your time, labour and money will be lost when plants become water-logged and die.

Fill the trough with a soil-based John Innes No. 3 potting compost – it will be worth the few pounds in order to produce a garden feature that will give you years of pleasure.

RAISED BEDS Raised beds are made most economically and simply from old bricks. Build two walls with a gap of 20–25 cm (8-10 in) between them and as high as you wish. About 60 cm (2 ft) is a useful height, although you might find that somewhat taller walls will be needed if the bed is to provide gardening for a disabled person. Be sure to leave drainage holes between the bricks at the foot of the walls. Fill the raised bed as for the trough.

JOBS FOR APRIL

GENERAL

If you find any bottles of chemical in your shed or garage that have lost their labels, don't try to economize by re-using them. It could well be false economy if what you thought was pesticide turns out to be weedkiller. Wash them away with plenty of water down any drain connected to the mains drainage system.

If you have a garden pool or water-tub garden (see p. 51), be sure that frogs have a way of crawling out of it. They commonly find their way in to lay spawn but then, without a ramp up which to crawl, they and their offspring are unable to escape. The main diet of frogs is slugs and they are among the gardener's greatest allies in the battle against pests – and they do it all for nothing.

THE INDOOR GARDEN

This is a good time to sow coleus seeds in pots. These most attractive foliage plants make beautiful and greatly appreciated gifts and are straightforward to grow.

Keep an eye open for the tell-tale signs of fluffy, white mealy bug on cacti and other house plants. They aren't easy to control but the simplest and cheapest way is by touching each colony with a paint-brush dipped in meths.

Primulas are popular house plants but the primrose-like varieties are all perfectly hardy outdoors. Around the beginning of April, I find that stores and garden centres are often selling off the remains of their winter stock and these lovely plants can then be obtained for little more than a few pence.

CONTAINERS

As daffodils and other bulbs fade in containers, continue to feed them. Don't lift them for drying until you are almost ready to put in their replacements, which with most summer bedding plants, won't be until the end of May. The old foliage may look unsightly for a time but it will be worthwhile tolerating this to ensure that your bulbs are big and plump enough to give you good flowers again next year.

Long term plants in containers such as shrubs or dwarf fruit trees should be given a good top dressing of general fertilizer at the beginning of the month, well watered and then mulched with compost.

✤ **'BUDGET TIP'** If you have a very large half barrel or similar big container full of compost that needs moving, don't risk causing yourself serious injury in the process. Contact a local builder or scaffolding company for three short lengths of old scaffolding pipe and roll the container on them. My experience has been that scaffolding pipe is the only readily available material remotely strong enough for the task.

GREENHOUSES, COLD FRAMES AND CLOCHES

Keep an eye out for the first signs of whitefly and aphids in the greenhouse and have a safe spray, such as one of the soap-based types, ready to deal with them promptly. Simply by being vigilant, you can save yourself much time and money later.

As tomato plants (and any aubergines or peppers sown earlier) continue to grow in their pots be sure they have good light and are supported by a small stick. Otherwise, they will be weak and elongated by the time they are planted out.

If you are planning to grow your 'indoor' crops in growing bags, be sure to bring the bags into the greenhouse or your porch about a couple of weeks before planting to allow the compost to warm up. Tomatoes especially don't like cold soil and it would be a pity to lose your precious plants by a little lack of care at this critical time.

APRIL

❋ **'BUDGET TIP'** If you find a spider in your bath or elsewhere in your home, don't kill it or even throw it into the garden. Pop it into a jar and bring it to your greenhouse where it will do invaluable, free work through the summer helping to keep the pests in check.

LAWN

The lawn is now due for its spring feed but, if you are using a fertilizer blend that includes a weedkiller (see p. 37), wait until the end of the month when the soil will be rather warmer. Lawn weedkillers don't work in cold conditions and at such times, will be a waste of money.

THE FLOWER GARDEN

Continue to sow hardy annual flower seeds outdoors. By sowing a few each week rather than all in one go, you will ensure that the flowering times are staggered and you will have effective garden displays for very much longer.

Cut down the foliage of garden bulbs about six weeks after the flowers have faded to be sure that the bulbs have had time to build up their strength for next year. Before you do so however, mark the position of each with a small stick – and if necessary, indicate the spot on your garden plan (see p. 8) – so that they aren't disturbed during your summer gardening activities.

As shoots elongate on herbaceous perennials such as delphiniums pull out the weaker ones to ensure the best display of flowers during summer.

Dahlia tubers should be planted outside towards the end of April. Put in a stick for support *before* you refill the planting hole – you will almost certainly spear the tubers and weaken your plants if you do it later. Plant gladiolus corms at convenient intervals for a truly cost-effective display.

❋ **'BUDGET TIP'** If you work on the assumption that gladioli take about 100 days from planting to flowering, you can virtually guarantee cut flowers for whatever week you choose later in the summer – very useful if you are planning a party, wedding or some other grand event.

At the end of the month, chrysanthemum plants that have been kept in a cold frame or other protection overwinter may safely be planted outside.

Any bulbs that have been lifted from the open ground or from containers should have the foliage cut off just above the bulb and then be dried carefully (not in full sun) for a week or two. Then they can be put in paper bags for storing in a cool, dry place until the autumn.

APRIL

✿ **'BUDGET TIP'** Remember to save paper bags from your shopping; they have plenty of uses in the garden.

By the middle of April, any moving and dividing of herbaceous perennials should be completed.

✿ **'BUDGET TIP'** A free and successful way to obtain new plants is to divide your own. You can swap any spares with friends and neighbours.

VEGETABLES

Continue to earth up early potatoes as the shoots emerge. If you are growing maincrop varieties, these may be safely planted around the middle of this month.

Towards the end of April you can switch from early to maincrop vegetable varieties.

With peas, you have a choice between several types of maincrop.

✿ **'BUDGET TIP'** An excellent pea variety (if you are prepared for something as tall as a runner bean) is 'Sugarsnap', for it offers two crops for the price of one. When young, they can be eaten like mange-tout; when mature the pods fill out like normal peas.

Continue to sow all types of hardy vegetables. Even if you have no cloches and haven't pre-warmed the soil, it will be safe to sow now in full expectation of good germination.

✿ **'BUDGET TIP'** There is no pest control cheaper or more effective than pinching out the tops of the overwintered variety of broad bean 'Aquadulce' in order to limit the attacks of the black bean aphid. And provided you do it before the aphids arrive the tops make a very tasty, tender and free green vegetable – cook them like spinach.

To ensure that you are efficient with your lettuce crops and don't alternate between glut and scarcity, sow a new row of seeds when the seedlings emerge from the previous sowing.

FRUIT

Check that raspberries and other cane fruits are carefully tied to their supports. Use soft string and make a figure of eight loop to ensure that the stem isn't constricted. If your plants have more than about seven canes each, cut out the weaker ones in order to allow the stronger to concentrate on producing the crop.

As apples and pears come into leaf, keep an eye open for any signs of mildew at the tips of the shoots, especially on young trees. Any that you

APRIL

spot should be pinched off carefully without showering the powdery white spores. In this way, you can very often keep the disease in check without any need for costly and time consuming spraying.

If you have strawberry crops in containers, or even in the open ground, throw some light netting over them towards the end of April to protect the flowers from sparrows, which seem to enjoy them almost as much as the fruit.

TREES AND SHRUBS

If you are growing standard trees or shrubs, keep an eye open for any signs of shoots emerging from the main stem. Rub or twist them out before they develop further and both weaken and disfigure the plant.

❀ **'BUDGET TIP'** When you visit your garden centre, don't forget to see if there are any cut-price offers. Frequently, trees and shrubs are sold at very much reduced prices once their flowers have faded and at this time of the year, it may be possible to pick up valuable and costly winter flowering varieties such as witch hazels relatively cheaply.

CLIMBERS

As you sow hardy and half hardy flower seeds don't forget the value of annual climbers for rapidly covering unsightly buildings or structures and giving you something almost instantly attractive and at almost no cost. Among my favourites are climbing nasturtiums, canary creeper, cup and saucer vine, *Eccremocarpus* and morning glory. All except nasturtiums should be sown in pots in warmth for hardening off and planting outdoors later.

SPRING GETS INTO ITS STRIDE

MAY

PLANT OF THE MONTH FOR MAY

Malus 'Golden Hornet' (Crab apple)

I AM ALL IN favour of plants that are both good to look at and good to eat. Crab apples fulfil these criteria admirably and, in the spring, they offer a wonderful spectacle with their blossom which according to the variety, can be white, pink or red. 'Golden Hornet' has star-like white flowers and then, later in the year, these develop small but beautiful, golden yellow fruits. As with all garden apples and related plants, the overall size of the tree can be selected very precisely by choosing an appropriate rootstock variety. In general crab apples are less prone to diseases than eating or cooking varieties and I never find that I have to spray mine during the summer, although I do give a tar oil spray in winter to eliminate overwintering aphids and other pests. A general fertilizer in spring and a compost mulch will help ensure that the tree gives the best return for your money.

J	F	M	A	M	J	J	A	S	O	N	D
							FR	FR	FR	FR	FR
		L	F	L	L	L	L	L			

F flowers, L leaves, Fr fruit, S stems [ ] denotes in some years

FEEDING YOUR PLANTS

By late spring young plants begin to remind you of young children – they need more and more to eat. For there are some things that you can safely leave to nature and some things that you can't. By and large, ensuring that your plants have enough food is one of those that you can't if you really want to obtain the best return for your efforts. Having spent time and money in obtaining the plants, the relatively small additional cost of

MAY

fertilizer will be amply repaid in the increased yield of edible plants and the immeasurably better show from your ornamentals. But you shouldn't feel that you need a whole armoury of different plant feeds. With two fertilizers only, you can cope with most situations; with three, pretty well everything.

SOLUBLE FERTILIZERS Soluble fertilizers can be used right through the summer for everything but will be especially important for your bedding plants and really fast-growing crops such as tomatoes. Plants in containers need feeding most of all because there is a finite amount of nutrient present in the potting compost, especially a soil-less type, and they will simply fade away if they aren't given additional feed after about six weeks. In general, you should apply soluble fertilizers at the dilutions recommended by the manufacturers once a week. The cost is minimal – the best known brand of general soluble fertilizer, Phostrogen, costs under £1 for sufficient to make 150 litres; although you could do even better by buying a 'bucket pack' and sharing with a group of friends – for around £11.50, you will have sufficient for 8000 litres (1760 gal) of feed.

❀ **'BUDGET TIP'** Do remember that buying fertilizers in large packs to be split up between a group of friends is perfectly legal but you *can't* and *mustn't* do it with pesticides.

GRANULAR FERTILIZERS Although soluble fertilizers can also be used for your house plants and, during summer, for your lawn, you will really benefit from also having one granular fertilizer. This is to use at planting time, before sowing and in spring and autumn when the temperatures aren't really warm enough for plants to absorb a soluble fertilizer very effectively. The cheapest and most useful general granular fertilizer is probably the organically based fish, blood and bone at between 50p and £1 per kilogram (2.2 lb), depending on the quantity in which you buy it. Growmore is a similarly priced, artificial equivalent but I find that it disappears from the soil rather more quickly.

If you do decide that you can stretch to buying a third type of fertilizer (and if you have a lawn) then a specially formulated, spring lawn feed should be your choice (see p. 37).

❀ **'BUDGET TIP'** Join your garden or allotment society. The subscription will be minimal but well worthwhile as you will be able to benefit from bulk purchases of fertilizers, seeds and other garden requirements, generally at very considerable savings. And of course the friendly community of fellow gardeners will be a wonderful free source of help, advice and indeed of plants too.

LAWN CARE

MAY

I know that when you come home from work, have cooking, washing or some other pressing task to do, mowing the lawn may appear like just one more in the seemingly endless list of chores. At such moments you may need convincing that a lawn is one of the least labour intensive yet attractive and inexpensive ways of gardening a given area of soil. But I do believe it to be true. After all, a lawn needs cutting only once a week, feeding once a year and you can just about get away without weeding it. Only if you have a very small garden that you need to walk across repeatedly in winter – causing the lawn to become unacceptably muddy – do I suggest that you adopt a 'physical' surface such as gravel instead of grass which although more expensive is almost maintenance-free.

You may be tempted by various types of lawn edging strip, made of plastic or metal and intended to keep the lawn edge neat and prevent the grass from creeping into the borders. I don't recommend them. They are difficult to install, can damage your mower and aren't very effective at their intended task. You will really do much better, and save yourself money, by using shears to clip the lawn edge and a spade to straighten it once a year in the early spring.

Lawn turf should be laid in a 'brick' pattern as shown here.

SEED OR TURF? New lawns can be made at any season of the year – provided the soil is fairly moist and not frozen – but the two best times are spring and early autumn. In making the decision as to whether to sow seed or lay turf you will need to assess the balance between the money and the time that you wish to spend. Sowing a lawn from seed is cheaper. Sufficient seed to sow 10 sq. m (12 sq. yd) will cost about £3. The equivalent in specially grown turf, delivered, could be six or eight times as much. The price can be reduced if you collect the turf; and, as with most things, reduced again if you club together with friends to buy a larger quantity.

✿ **'BUDGET TIP'** If you really need only a very small amount, less than 6 sq. m (7 sq. yd) say, it might be worth ringing a local landscaping contractor who may well have oddments left over from a large job.

But whatever you do, resist the temptation to buy cheap 'meadow turf' from the small ad columns; it will be full of weeds and fine for grazing cattle but not much else.

A lawn grown from seed, however, will take you longer – it will need regular watering (not easy if you have a hosepipe ban and so can't use a sprinkler), bird protection netting (itself an extra cost) or scarers, and hand weeding since there are no chemical weedkillers suitable for newly sown lawns. Such a lawn will also take much longer to establish – it will be at least six weeks before you can walk on it and considerably longer before it can be used for football or other children's activities. A turfed lawn is instant – but at a price.

If you do, however, decide to sow a lawn, there are several things to remember. Dig the area very thoroughly beforehand, taking care especially to remove any perennial weeds – it is much easier now than later. Rake the surface very carefully just before you sow and try to rake in two directions at right angles to avoid having any humps and hollows. Just before the final raking, scatter some *autumn* lawn fertilizer over the surface to help the new grass to establish. Don't buy more seed than you need – work out your total area and look at the packets to see how much each will cover. But don't try to economize by buying bulk seed from un-named bags; you will always obtain better germination and better grass from a branded packet.

The packet will indicate the density of sowing – either by providing a small measure to use for each square metre or sometimes by giving a picture showing the appearance of the grass on the surface. After sowing, rake again very gently so the seed is just buried and then firm it by walking over the entire surface, but be careful not to leave deep heel prints. Although I have said that bird netting is expensive, don't be tempted to economize by erecting black cotton over the area as this will trap birds' legs. You can, however, make other home-made bird scarers; anything that flaps is the most effective and small strips cut from coloured plastic bags are fairly good.

If you are turfing your lawn, the basic soil preparation and fertilizer are the same as for seed and if you are having your turves delivered, try to have them dropped as close as possible to the prepared area as they are fiendishly heavy to carry. Lay the turves off-set, like bricks in a wall. At the end of the row, you will almost certainly find you have to cut the turf and may well be left with a very small piece. But don't leave this at the end of the row where it will fray and tear away; instead, pull a full-sized turf to the end and drop the short piece in behind it. Tamp the turves down carefully with a block of wood, but again, be careful not to leave heel prints.

MAY

LAWNMOWERS When caring for a lawn the only real priority is a mower. There is now a wide range for every imaginable type of lawn but, in my experience, the choice for a small garden lawn really comes down to two or three inexpensive ones, all electric. Most lawns will be well served by a small, wheeled rotary, preferably with a grass collector box. If your lawn is on a slope or is very irregular, you might just prefer a hover mower, the cheaper models of which will not have a grass collector. If you become very keen and really begin to take a serious pride in your turf, try a small cylinder model which will give a closer cut and produce those appealing stripes.

Prices for a new hover or rotary mower start at about £50 – rather more for a cylinder model – but these are really academic because it is almost always possible to buy mowers second-hand.

Left: an example of an electric rotary mower. *Right:* an electric cylinder mower.

❀ **'BUDGET TIP'** Try to have a second-hand mower checked by an electrician – preferably before you pay for it.

Always ensure an electric mower has a safety cut out device (technically called a residual current-operated circuit breaker). These can be obtained from DIY stores and should of course be used with all other electric tools and appliances.

You may well see second-hand push mowers for sale very cheaply. If all else fails they are worth trying but you really do need a good dry lawn and well-sharpened mower blades to make cutting the grass other than very hard and frustrating work.

LAWN RAKES A lawn will also benefit from raking in late autumn and again in early spring with a spring-tine rake. This will clear away twigs, leaves, worm casts and other debris and pull out some of the 'thatch' of dead grass and moss. This task can be done only with a spring-tine rake and I recommend this type of rake, rather than a rigid garden rake, for general use – there's no point in having two tools when you can manage with one (but see p. 121).

MAY

CONTAINER GARDENING

The fact that plants can be grown in containers is nothing new – the Romans did it. By and large though they did it for effect, not for its rather more valuable dimension of enabling you to garden in very little space and, if you are prepared to improvise, at almost no cost. For whilst the variety of purpose-made containers has never been greater, or cheaper, thanks to the advent of moulded plastic, there are so many types today that can be turned to gardening advantage:

- Old paint tins
- Car tyres
- Barrels
- Bowls and buckets
- Babies' baths
- Saucepans
- Wellington boots

The possibilities are almost limitless; you simply need to ensure that there is some form of drainage in the bottom. But the effects can be dramatic – an old saucepan with pale blue lobelia tumbling over the sides, a pile of tyres producing a bumper crop of courgettes and a chimney pot sprouting forth nasturtiums. Let your imagination run riot. The subject of chimney pots reminds me that one of the budget gardener's best friends can be a local builder. He may well have old chimneys, wood, bricks, window frames, even small quantities of top soil – all for the trouble of taking them from his skip.

A few other tips:
- Do wash out containers before you re-use them; and
- If you garden on a tower block balcony, be sure that you know the load restrictions that apply: 1 cu. m (1.3 cu. yd) of potting compost weighs 1 tonne (1 ton). It would be most unfortunate to find your planted containers delivered, unannounced, to the people on the ground floor.

POTTING COMPOST Your container gardening will only be successful if you use a proper potting compost. For plants, being grown for one season only, any general purpose compost will suffice. Longer-term plants however need a soil-based John Innes No. 3 potting compost, which is excellent value for money as the same compost with the addition of a little fertilizer will suffice for many years.

❀ **'BUDGET TIP'** If you plan to use a very large container, such as a half-

MAY

barrel, you can economize by half filling it with a mixture of good garden soil and old bricks or stones (not mortar rubble) and then topping up with the potting compost.

One special type of container that has become very important in recent years is the plastic growing bag, filled with soil-less compost and used principally for growing tomatoes. You can however use it for bedding plants, lettuces or pretty well any other annuals too. Growing bags have certainly revolutionized gardening for many people with no real garden at all, for they can be placed on concrete paths, paved areas, even on balconies on tower blocks. To obtain the best value from your growing bag, grow only the number of plants that the manufacturers recommend for the size of bag. And as with all soil-less compost, you must begin to apply liquid fertilizer after about six weeks.

❀ **'BUDGET TIP'** When the plants in a growing bag are finished try re-using the bag for a late crop of winter lettuce or winter flowering pansies. Provided your main plants have not had any disease the second 'crop' should grow well, but they *must* be given a liquid fertilizer as that in the compost itself will have been exhausted.

WATER FEATURES

Unless you have been fortunate enough to acquire one with your existing garden, you are unlikely to want to go to the trouble and cost of constructing a full-sized garden pool. And in any event, if you have young children, it isn't a garden feature that I would really recommend – a youngster can drown in a very few centimetres of water.

But there's no denying that some water in a garden can be extremely attractive and appealing and, if the idea of a few fish, a water lily and one or two other modest pond plants appeals to you, what about a tub garden? There is no more inexpensive and easy way of bringing the pleasure of water into your garden and May or June are the ideal months in which to start.

All you need is a wooden half-barrel, which can be obtained very readily.

❀ **'BUDGET TIP'** Wooden half-barrels are generally much cheaper when bought through the small ads or directly from breweries than through a garden centre.

MAY

Do be sure however that you obtain a genuine beer or cider barrel that has been cut in half. It is sometimes possible to obtain made-up barrels but these will always leak.

Having obtained your barrel, wash and scrub it thoroughly inside and stop up any bung or tap hole. Then place it in a sunny position, and the one in which it is to stay – you will not be able to move it again once it is full. Raise it on old bricks to prevent it rotting on the outside. Ideally, it should be allowed to fill with rain water but tap water will do at a pinch. Place a few bricks inside to create platforms at different levels for your plants which should be grown in plastic baskets, obtainable at any good garden centre.

Regarding plants, you will need:
● One small water lily;
● Perhaps two other *small* pond plants – the garden centre will advise you which of their stock will not be too vigorous;
● A couple of bunches of submerged oxygenating plants; and perhaps
● Three small fish.

My personal suggestions for plants in a small pool would be the oxygenating plant hornwort (*Ceratophyllum demersum*), the water lily 'Pygmaea Alba', and the pond plants water forget-me-not (*Myosotis scorpioides*) and golden club (*Orontium aquaticum*).

Such a feature will not only give you hours of very inexpensive enjoyment but also your children an education in miniature as they watch the water life come and go.

JOBS FOR MAY

GENERAL

As soon as any signs of the green 'cotton wool' of blanket weed appear in your pool or water-tub garden, pull it out by hand after rolling up your sleeve.

Don't forget to feed the fish regularly with a proprietary fish food – a small packet will last all season in a small pool.

If you have trouble with mice and voles in your garden you may well find that an old-fashioned mouse trap is a good investment. But always be sure that the trap is covered so that birds aren't caught by it.

THE INDOOR GARDEN

I'm sure that the house plant producers are kept in business more by people losing plants through having put them in the wrong place than by anything else. I also find that the advice given on labels and in house plant books is often too generalized. Much the best plan is to move your house plants around your home, leaving them in each place for a couple of weeks at a time. They will tell you which place they prefer by how well they grow there.

Even though outdoor growing conditions are now good, the window sill collection of herbs is still very useful for its convenience – and especially so if you have little or no real garden.

❀ **'BUDGET TIP' For about £4–5, you can grow a pretty comprehensive herb collection from seed and plants. And if this sounds expensive, look at the price of a few sprigs of fresh herbs next time you are in the supermarket.**

CONTAINERS

At the end of May you may safely plant up containers of all types with half-hardy bedding plants – provided they have been adequately hardened off. If you are buying plants from a garden centre don't assume they have been accustomed to outdoor conditions already; give them a week or ten days hardening off before planting.

If you have little or no real garden, don't forget the value of growing bags for bedding plants. In a single growing bag on the edge of a patio, a mixture of a dozen plants such as petunias, lobelia, alyssum and marigolds will give you a wonderful display at very little cost.

❀ **'BUDGET TIP' Club together with a friend if you find it difficult to buy some types of plants in odd ones – quite often garden centres sell a minimum of half a dozen of each type – or ask the garden centre if they have any damaged trays of plants that they will let you have very cheaply.**

GREENHOUSES, COLD FRAMES AND CLOCHES

Greenhouse fruits such as tomatoes, aubergines and peppers can now be planted in their growing positions. Gardeners often have difficulty staking them in growing bags but, instead of buying one of the expensive purpose-made frames, insert a cane into the soil or attach it to the side of the greenhouse behind the bag and then train the stem along a small cane placed diagonally from the base of the plant to the vertical cane. Use soft garden string to tie the two canes together.

Once the seed trays are cleared from the shelves, use your greenhouse as a 'hospital' for any ailing house plants. By pulling away damaged or yellowed leaves, giving them a liquid feed and keeping them in good light for a few weeks, the improvement can be remarkable and you will be saved the cost of buying a replacement.

MAY

To avoid giving a check in growth to your tomatoes, don't water them with water directly from the tap. Place the watering can in the greenhouse or porch to give the water a chance to warm up.

Once the cold frame is free from plants being hardened off, why not fill it with a melon sown in a large pot filled with a mixture of garden compost and soil. The variety 'Sweetheart' is excellent for a small space.

LAWN

If you have a mower with adjustable cutters, they may now be lowered slightly, provided that the grass is beginning to dry out and the weather isn't very wet.

❀ **'BUDGET TIP'** Use an old fork as in improvised weed grubber – there is no cheaper way of removing clump-forming lawn weeds such as daisies and plantain.

The beginning of May is an excellent time for planting or sowing a new lawn, provided the soil has been well prepared (see p. 47).

THE FLOWER GARDEN

If when you are planting out your summer bedding plants, you find that the winter bedding pansies are still in good bloom, don't waste them. Pot up a few for bringing into the house where they will give you several weeks of attractive flowers.

Continue to sow hardy annual flower seeds outdoors, as in April. For delicious perfume on summer evenings buy a packet of mignonette seed and sow a few among your other plants. The flowers aren't anything special to look at, but their presence will soon be evident.

Continue to stake and tie in herbaceous perennials as they elongate. If you leave it too late their stems will flop and you will lose the value and impact of the plants for the whole summer.

Make sure that sweet pea plants don't dry out – water them thoroughly and then, if you haven't already done so, apply a layer of compost mulch around them. Moisture is essential not only for good growth but also to limit attacks of mildew, thus avoiding costly chemical sprays.

Pinch out the tips of recently planted bedding plants once they are established. This will help to encourage bushier growth and so give you many more flowers for your money.

Keep an eye out for weed growth among your newly sown plants – it can take practice to distinguish them from the flowers but you will need to

MAY

pull out the weeds by hand in order to give your plants a chance to establish properly.

Lupins are prone to attack by a large, aggressive species of aphid which is very difficult to control. Be prepared to spray at the first signs of attack therefore for they can reduce your plants to a pathetic state in very little time.

When the flowers have faded on tulips, the bulbs should be lifted, while still in leaf, and replanted temporarily in a corner of the garden until the foliage has finally died down (but see my notes on choice of tulips on p. 105).

❀ **'BUDGET TIP'** In your beds and borders look out for self-sown seedlings of annuals grown last year and perennials such as hellebores and aquilegias. Carefully transplant these free gifts to where they will give the best display.

VEGETABLES

If you are planning to sow runner beans directly outside, this may safely be done by mid-May in the knowledge that the young shoots are unlikely to be frosted. The best, tastiest and most prolific variety that I grow is the stringless 'Polestar'.

❀ **'BUDGET TIP'** When you erect your wigwam or tent style arrangement of canes for runner beans, you can cut down the costs appreciably by missing out every second and third cane and using string or garden twine, pegged to the ground instead.

By mid-month too, you can sow outdoor ridge cucumbers and courgettes. One plant of each will be adequate for most families and, if you use bush varieties of courgette, they will take up relatively little room. Cucumbers can be trained up sticks or canes to save space and so save money. Choose 'King of the Ridge' for a cucumber with flavour even better than the expensive supermarket types and 'Gold Rush' for a very prolific golden-coloured courgette. Remember that if you allow one or two courgettes to grow into marrows, you will have two types of vegetable for the price of one. Both cucumbers and courgettes can also be raised in growing bags but they do require a great deal of watering.

Continue also to sow all types of hardy maincrop vegetables. If you have a light soil and have trouble (as I do) with spinach running to seed, try two variants – perpetual spinach and Swiss chard, both of which are less likely to bolt. Swiss chard is another cost-saving dual-role vegetable. You can use the green parts as spinach and the white mid-ribs as a substitute for asparagus – although the taste is rather different.

MAY

Sow a few pot marigolds among your vegetables. They look most attractive and their orange flowers are edible so they too have a double function. And I think they help to keep down aphids by attracting hoverflies, whose larvae eat aphids.

FRUIT

Keep an eye out for any signs of sawfly larvae (small, dark greenish, caterpillar-like creatures) on gooseberries, red and white (but not black-) currants. Nip off any by hand and be prepared to use a safe, soap-based spray if they persist. They can strip a plant of its foliage within a few days.

If your strawberries are in big pots or in the open ground, the fruits will need some protection from contact with the soil to prevent rotting.

❀ **'BUDGET TIP'** Although straw is ideal, old plastic bags placed under strawberries will also protect fruits from contact with the soil.

TREES AND SHRUBS

Lightly prune spring flowering shrubs such as broom and berberis as the flowers fade. On older, very woody plants up to one third of the oldest branches may be cut out completely.

Keep an eye open for the first signs of aphids, mildew or blackspot on roses and spray promptly when they appear. By using a combined pest and disease spray you will save on both cost and time.

CLIMBERS

Carefully tie in climbers of all types, both annual and perennial, as their shoots elongate. Even self-clinging types may need some help initially if they are to flourish and earn their keep. Ivy however is an exception – it will climb only when it is ready – so be prepared for it to form a mound of growth first at the foot of the wall or other support.

EARLY SUMMER SPLENDOUR

JUNE

PLANT OF THE MONTH FOR JUNE

Rosa **'Aloha' (Rose)**

'A LOHA' IS A rose that flowers reliably through most of the summer and well into the start of winter and for me, is almost the perfect modern rose. It is a short climber (about 2 m/6 ft 6 in) but it could also be grown as a tall shrub. It has rich pink, very double, fragrant flowers offset against lush dark green foliage. Apart from a brief period in late July in some seasons, mine can be relied on to be in bloom for five months. 'Aloha' is also a trouble-free plant for I never have to spray it against mildew, rust, blackspot or aphids, and so is ideal if you are busy. As with other roses, it will always be best in a moisture-retentive soil, either a heavy clay or a lighter one that has had plenty of compost or other organic matter dug in.

J	F	M	A	M	J	J	A	S	O	N	D
					F	F	F	F	F	F	

F flowers, L leaves, Fr fruit, S stems [ ] denotes in some years

ORGANIZING A VEGETABLE GARDEN

On average, fresh vegetables make up at least 10 per cent of every family's weekly grocery bill and, even if you are able to supply only part of your requirements for part of the year, the savings can be remarkable. And I'm sure everyone agrees that vegetables picked or dug freshly from your own plot taste so much better than any that you buy. You can select the best flavoured varieties too and these are very often different from those that commercial growers produce.

Very few of us have the space, time or indeed the inclination to try and become self-sufficient in home-grown produce. I suggest therefore

JUNE

that first you draw up a list of the vegetables that your family prefers and grade them for cost. These costs of course will vary from one time of the year to another and bear in mind that I am only concerned with *fresh* not frozen or canned produce, but a glance along your supermarket or greengrocer's shelves will soon reveal that salad crops, peas and beans, cauliflowers, calabrese, spinach, carrots, onions, new potatoes, Brussels sprouts and 'luxury' items such as aubergines, endives and courgettes will be among the most costly. At the cheaper end will be old (main crop) potatoes, swedes, turnips, parsnips, cabbage, curly kale and purple sprouting broccoli (as opposed to calabrese).

We have a working list therefore in the more expensive items and the next step is to eliminate those that take up a great deal of room and/or are particularly tricky or time-consuming to grow. On these counts I would remove Brussels sprouts and cauliflowers and also, if your soil is very heavy, carrots although they are fine for lighter soils. Although new potatoes take up a fair amount of space they are well worth including as they are important in crop rotation. This is the key to growing vegetables well and it simply means trying to move your crops around year by year so that the same type of plant isn't grown on the same soil more than one year in three.

✿ **'BUDGET TIP'** Crops that are rotated grow much better than those planted in the same site each year, and they therefore earn their keep more by giving higher yields.

CROP ROTATION For the purposes of rotation vegetables are usually arranged in three groups. In limited space and with the crops I have short-listed, I suggest that these groups are:

● Root vegetables (carrots and new potatoes);
● Peas and beans, and
● The rest.

The ideal is to grow sufficient in each group to occupy roughly an equal area of ground and to swap them around so that it is three years before each group comes back to the same area.

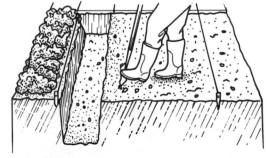

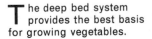
The deep bed system provides the best basis for growing vegetables.

58

DEEP BEDS Much the best way of growing vegetables to obtain the most profitable yield and also to save on time is by the deep bed system. Divide your vegetable garden into beds, each approximately 1.2 m (4 ft) wide and as long as space allows. Each of these beds should be double dug (see p. 11) and should not then be walked on at all. The bed width is such that sowing, planting, hoeing, weeding and harvesting can either be done from the sides or from a 'bridge' made from a plank resting on two bricks set at either side.

ROSES FOR THE GARDEN

Roses represent excellent value; modern mass production means that you can buy good quality plants for only a couple of pounds and, if you choose your varieties carefully, you can have flowers more or less right through summer. Roses also require little attention – just a pruning in spring and an annual feed with a general fertilizer (see p. 45). One or two sprays against pests and diseases may be needed (see p. 67), although careful choice of varieties with some resistance to attack will save money here too.

No garden can be complete without some roses. Although tradition-ally thought of as plants for clay soils, they will in fact thrive in most conditions provided organic matter is dug in to improve moisture retentiveness. One complaint often made is that they have nothing to offer in winter when they are little better than a bunch of bare twigs. This may be important when they are grown in beds to the exclusion of all other plants but grow them, as I do, in odd ones among other plants in your border and their winter bareness will be insignificant.

❀ **'BUDGET TIP'** For the best return in terms of length of flowering time choose modern hybrid tea and floribunda rose varieties – most of the older shrub types bloom for a relatively short period and also tend to be pretty big plants. The same is true of climbing roses – the climbing versions of the modern varieties will be a better bet.

If you have no garden or very limited space some roses make good subjects for growing in containers: the miniatures or slightly larger patio varieties are considerably shorter-growing than more conventional types yet have a great deal of charm. Like most plants in containers they require a little more attention – an occasional liquid feed during summer and care in not allowing the compost to dry out are especially important.

To help you through the maze of the thousands of rose varieties that exist and even the several dozen that you will see at the average garden centre, I have drawn up my recommended list for small, budget gardens. My top 12 roses should all be widely available and offer, I think, the best return in value for money, flowering, vigour, disease and pest resistance and weather tolerance.

JUNE

Roses for small, budget gardens

CULTIVAR	TYPE OF ROSE	FEATURES
R. 'Alec's Red'	Hybrid Tea	Red, fragrant
R. 'Aloha'	Low climber	Pink, fragrant, masses of flowers, and disease resistant
R. 'Arthur Bell'	Floribunda	Yellow, some fragrance, good rain and disease resistance
R. 'Easter Morning'	Miniature	Ivory, beautiful form
R. 'Iceberg'	Floribunda or climber	White, some fragrance
R. 'Korresia'	Floribunda	Yellow, masses of flowers
R. 'Maigold'	Climber	Peach-orange, masses of flowers early in the season
R. 'Masquerade'	Floribunda	Yellow changing to pink and then red
R. 'Parkdirektor Riggers'	Climber	Red, semi-double, masses of flowers, some fragrance
R. 'Perle d'Or'	Low shrub	Small apricot flowers of perfect form
R. 'Queen Elizabeth'	Floribunda	For larger gardens, masses of superb pink flowers
R. 'Silver Jubilee'	Hybrid Tea	Silvery pink with peach shades, fragrant

AN INSTANT GARDEN

There are occasions in life when we simply haven't had time to plan our gardens in advance. Perhaps we've just moved house, or perhaps there have been more pressing things to occupy us. Then spring and summer arrive and there is nothing to colour our surroundings. Clearly you can't create something instantly without some outlay so set yourself a strict budget of how much you are prepared to spend and then take a little time at the garden centre to see how you can obtain the best value.

HARDY ANNUALS The cheapest plants are those that can be sown from seed outdoors in late spring and still produce a good display within the year. Most are hardy annuals and among them, you will have the best results from alyssum, pot marigolds, candytuft, nasturtium (the climbing form is excellent for covering an area in poor soil), nemesia and, of course, don't forget sunflowers. You can also sow a number of vegetables in expectation of a crop within weeks:

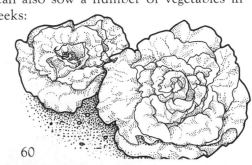

● Radishes, which are well known for growing quickly;
● Varieties of small lettuce such as 'Tom Thumb'; (*right*)
● Stump-rooted carrots;
● Courgettes (marrows);

JUNE

- French beans;
- Spinach; and
- Early varieties of peas and beetroot (which are quick growing).

❀ **'BUDGET TIP'** The budget gardener should avoid slow growing plants such as brassicas and onions, which will provide only one crop in the same time that two quick-growing plants can be productive.

You will be lucky to fill your garden entirely from a late start with seed-raised plants. You may need to buy in some plants from a garden centre. But do choose carefully. Trays of bedding annuals are tempting, but if you can afford only a couple, select those that will put on plenty of growth. The following are good value:

- Petunias are good provided the season isn't dull and wet;
- Lobelia is lovely for edging and the trailing varieties will bulk up considerably; and
- African marigolds will individually become very large and colourful plants during the course of the summer.

QUICK-GROWING HERBACEOUS PERENNIALS Ideally you should put some of your money into plants that will still be there when summer has gone. Among quick growing herbaceous perennials which give excellent value for money by flowering twice – once in summer and again next spring – you will do no better than with some of the hardy geraniums; choose taller types such as the red flowered *Geranium psilostemon* or the lilac *G.* × *oxonianum* 'Claridge Druce'. Among other quick growing perennials to give good 'instant garden' value are:

- Ligularias (for wetter soils)
- Hostas (*right*)
- *Campanula glomerata*
- Crocosmias
- Euphorbias
- Hemerocallis (day lilies) and
- Black-eyed Susan (*Rudbeckia*)

BULBS Don't forget bulbs for their almost instant value. In the early part of the year, they are sold already flowering in pots.

❀ **'BUDGET TIP'** As spring progresses, pot-grown bulbs in flower can often be bought relatively cheaply – and of course can then be planted in the garden after the flowers have faded.

JUNE

Remember that the best visual effects will be achieved if limited numbers of plants are concentrated together. Don't scatter your bedding plants here and there but group them in an eye-catching manner close to the house.

PATIOS AND BARBECUES

You can best enjoy a garden when you are actually in it. For me there is no pleasure simply in staring through the windows at what I have achieved. You need somewhere outside to sit and enjoy yourself.

Garden furniture can be obtained inexpensively but undoubtedly the best time to buy it is in late summer when stores are clearing their stock. Choose tables and chairs that can be folded for storage. Left out overwinter, any garden furniture will deteriorate and soon need replacing.

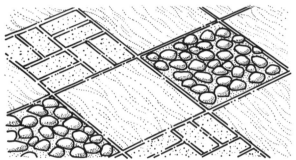

Paving can be made more interesting by replacing some slabs with pebbles or a brick pattern as shown here.

PATIOS The sitting-out area must be big enough to accommodate the table and chairs without people falling off the edges. And although you can make do with gravel over a soil surface, furniture will inevitably sink in. A hard surface is immeasurably better and second-hand concrete slabs offer much the best value. Unfortunately, they are very heavy; loading more than an odd one into your car could cause harm to both you and the vehicle. If the supplier can't deliver therefore, it will be worthwhile finding a local 'man with a van'. The notion of unrelieved concrete slabs may strike you as boring, so try replacing the odd slab with a pattern of old bricks or even of flat cobbles set in mortar. You will be amazed how just such a little variety will bring life to the patio.

BARBECUES Set aside an area for a barbecue to encourage more summer outdoor living. The Hibachi type tends to be the cheapest proprietary barbecue and can be raised to a working level on old bricks. But do be sure that they are secure; an unstable barbecue is a dangerous toy. And do site the barbecue away from overhanging shrubs or trees that could easily be ignited by flying sparks.

❧ **'BUDGET TIP'** A reasonably efficient DIY enthusiast could make a barbecue from bricks or concrete blocks with a strong metal grid. But do be sure that you are using fire tolerant bricks or blocks as others may split with the heat, and don't be tempted to try and make it too big – you will never heat it all thoroughly enough.

JUNE

JOBS FOR JUNE

GENERAL

Try to visit as many public gardens and parks as you can during the summer. One of the best sources of free ideas is to see the way that other people have tackled problems, but even better is to be able to talk to the gardeners themselves. *Gardens of England and Wales* (often known as the Yellow Book) lists private gardens that open to the public on one or two days each year and a copy will be in your local library. (There are also Scottish and Irish volumes.) The admission charge to these gardens averages only about 75p (in aid of worthy charities) and teas are often available very inexpensively. Also many garden owners have plants for sale at budget prices too. All in all, it can make a very low cost and enjoyable day out for the family.

THE INDOOR GARDEN

Most woody house plants (including the most popular ones, azaleas) should be put outside in a warm but slightly shaded spot for the summer. If you have a fairly acid soil, then their pots may be sunk in it up to the rim. Remember to water them and give liquid feed several times during the coming weeks.

CONTAINERS

Container plants of all types will now be growing vigorously. They will need watering and if they are in a soil-less compost, they will be in need of feeding too. Apply a general purpose liquid feed (see p. 45) once a week.

As garden centres move from spring into summer, you will find that, as at all seasonal changes, the previous season's stock may be sold off cheaply.

❀ **'BUDGET TIP'** June is the month to look out for cut-price growing bags. Sometimes a mere puncture can cut the cost almost to nothing. A few left over bedding plants will be there for a song too and, as I suggested in May, the combination can be very effective.

❀ **'BUDGET TIP'** A cheap and effective way to repair a hole in a growing bag is with waterproof sticky tape.

JUNE

GREENHOUSES, COLD FRAMES AND CLOCHES

At the beginning of June, the last of the cloches should be removed from any plants outdoors. Their job is finished for this summer but wash them carefully and store them ready for use again in the autumn.

Tomatoes will be growing vigorously and must have their side shoots pinched out if they are to give of their best. Use your finger and thumb to pinch out all of the shoots that arise from the sides of the stem – and keep a special eye open for those that lurk hidden around the back. Keep tying the main stem regularly to its support cane too.

If insect pest populations begin to build up in the greenhouse, hang up sticky yellow cards (they are inexpensive and obtainable from garden centres) which will trap them most effectively. Try to avoid leaning over your plants as you will find the cards also stick very firmly to your hair.

LAWN

The mower can be set even lower, but don't overdo it and shave the grass. If you cut too low – below 1 cm (½ in) – this will allow moss to develop.

Even if the weather is very dry, don't be tempted to water the lawn. It is a waste of time, effort and water for grass always recovers after drought – whereas your other garden plants may not.

If you do use a weedkiller on your lawn (see p. 37), allow four days without mowing before you apply it and four days again afterwards. And don't use compost made from lawn mowings containing weedkiller until it has been in the compost bin for six months.

THE FLOWER GARDEN

❀ **'BUDGET TIP'** If you have a fairly large garden, it is well worthwhile sowing spring bedding plants such as wallflowers and sweet williams in the vegetable plot or other convenient spot. They are slow growing and rather big plants that must be transplanted in the autumn and will not flower until next spring. By raising your own, they will be very much cheaper than the plants that you would otherwise need to buy before the winter.

Just because annuals are small plants, and often bear a very large number of flowers, don't neglect dead-heading them. Just as with roses and other large ornamentals, dead-heading will encourage the production of more blooms and so give you the very best value.

Do pick sweet peas regularly for the house. Not only are they the finest of all flowers for cutting, but also they will tend to stop blooming if some flowers are allowed to set seed.

JUNE

With tall-growing herbaceous perennials such as delphiniums, you will need to re-stake them as they grow upwards, replacing short with slightly longer canes each time. There is nothing finer than a straight, upright delphinium – and nothing worse than a kinked one.

Most herbaceous border plants are divided in spring or autumn, but an exception is the tall border iris. Every four or five years these lovely plants should be divided in June, immediately after they have flowered. When replanting them bury the rhizomes only very shallowly, leaving the top parts exposed to the sun.

Plant a few 'St Brigid' or 'De Caen' anemones at intervals over the next few weeks. A packet of corms is very inexpensive and in return, you will have a succession of lovely, bright flowers well into the autumn.

Your dahlias should be growing well by the end of the month and you then have two choices: if you want a few large flowers for a special display, pinch out some of the side buds. If you want masses of small flowers for cutting, however, then let them all develop.

Some of the early spring flowering plants such as aquilegias and doronicums will now not only have finished flowering but may well, by the end of the month, also be succumbing to mildew. However, don't bother trying to spray them. In order to keep them vigorous for next year, cut down all of the top growth. New, healthy foliage will arise again before autumn.

VEGETABLES

The beginning of June is the half-hardy plant's all-clear because for almost all of the British Isles, the danger of frost is now past so runner beans, tomatoes and all other tender vegetables may be planted outside. And those sown outdoors in May can now safely show their heads above the soil.

❀ **'BUDGET TIP'** Wherever you have room and wherever plants from earlier sowings of hardy annuals have been removed, sow some more. Bare soil is simply money going to waste.

Vegetables will be needing water throughout the summer (see p. 77).

❀ **'BUDGET TIP'** A good way to economize on water is to cut the bottom off plastic drink bottles and then half bury them, top downwards, in the soil among your crops. When filled with water the bottles will act as slow-release reservoirs, gradually allowing the water to seep out into the root zone where it is most needed.

Look out for caterpillars on your plants, especially if you grow members of the cabbage family. No spray is needed, you can simply pick them off

JUNE

by hand (using gloves is a good idea as some caterpillars have irritating hairs).

Continue to earth up potatoes, not this time to protect the shoots from frost but to ensure that the tubers are covered with soil. Exposed to the light, they turn green and highly poisonous.

FRUIT

Pull out any raspberry suckers that appear at some distance from the main plants. If allowed to remain they will weaken the fruiting shoots and so reduce yields.

Once you have picked your strawberry crop, trim over the plants with shears or scissors to encourage new growth. If you are growing a mixture of varieties, be sure not to trim the later ones accidentally before they have fruited.

If weeding between the canes of soft fruit, be careful not to hoe too close to the plants for they have shallow roots which are easily damaged.

TREES AND SHRUBS

By the second half of June most roses should have had their first flush of blooms and with a little attention, will produce more during the summer. Dead-head them regularly by cutting each dead flower head back to just above the first outward-facing bud with five, not three, leaflets. Ideally, they should then be given a handful of general fertilizer.

Check the ties on young trees. With rapid growth during the summer, the ties can soon become very tight.

You can produce new plants from shrubs, even from evergreens and those other types that are difficult to propagate with cuttings, by layering them. Choose a low-hanging branch and peg it down into the soil. Place a rock or other large weight on top and be patient. Within a year, it should have rooted and can then be separated from the parent plant to give you another one free of charge.

CLIMBERS

Continue to tie in any wayward shoots on climbers of all types – do be careful to pull away any growth that threatens to penetrate beneath roof tiles or into wooden window frames. A little bit of tidying up now could save you a great deal of expense later.

BALMY DAYS

PLANT OF THE MONTH FOR JULY

Geranium × *oxonianum* **'Claridge Druce' (Cranesbill)**

I AM THE WORLD'S greatest fan of hardy geraniums. They sum up so many of the trouble-free features desired in modern gardening whilst offering flowers for long periods and usually other attributes too. I would commend them all but have singled out 'Claridge Druce' for gardeners wanting a pretty, vigorous ground cover for parts of the garden they may not have time to turn over to neatly tended beds and borders. It bears lilac flowers throughout the summer and self-seeds readily, spreading to provide weed-smothering ground cover. An individual plant will form a clump of about 45 × 45 cm (18 × 18 in) within a season. Any cranesbill seedlings not wanted can easily be pulled out and given to friends with similar gardening needs. Cut back the foliage in autumn and divide it every two or three years or simply allow it to extend and turn unattractive waste ground into something very pleasing.

J	F	M	A	M	J	J	A	S	O	N	D
			L	L	F	F	F	F	F	F	

F flowers, L leaves, Fr fruit, S stems [ ] denotes in some years

PROTECTING YOUR PLANTS AGAINST PESTS AND DISEASES

Your hard-earned investment in garden plants can be lost more quickly to the jaws of caterpillars and the sap-sucking activities of greenfly than to anything else. And it is at the height of summer's warmth – usually in July – that garden pests are at their busiest. But this needn't mean that your garden must be drenched with expensive and unpleasant chemicals – just a little care, attention and vigilance can save you pounds.

KEEPING THE GARDEN NEAT AND TIDY I have always believed that a neat and tidy garden is more likely to be a healthy one than if it is cluttered with rubbish and debris. A simple walk around your garden collecting together piles of old prunings, old and rotting seed boxes and sundry

JULY

other debris will be time extremely well spent because it is on and among such remains that many pests – slugs, snails and woodlice most notably – will hide. Some fungus diseases can live on dead and rotting remains too and spread from there to infect your precious plants. Such rubbish should be bagged and taken to the local tip; or, if you are lucky, left for your local authority to collect. Cleanliness may or may not be next to godliness but it is certainly the hallmark of a wise and thrifty gardener.

COMMON PROBLEMS AND SOLUTIONS You can protect your plants and also save on sprays simply by appreciating the conditions in which some of the commonest problems thrive. Among diseases mildew flourishes in hot dry conditions and for this reason is often common on climbers and other plants growing on walls. Be sure that these plants are well-watered and well-mulched therefore in order to keep the atmosphere around them cool and moist. By contrast the fluffy grey mould that so often causes decay to plants in cold frames and greenhouses towards the end of summer likes moist, cool conditions. Its impact can be minimized by ensuring that the structure has good ventilation. For rather a similar reason most diseases in the garden can be discouraged by placing your plants well apart. To do otherwise results in stagnant, damp air. Read your seed packet instructions on spacing carefully – trying to cram in more plants than are recommended is false economy.

Make nature save money for you by encouraging natural predators. Ladybird and hoverfly larvae for example will eat prodigious quantities of aphids and these and other friendly insects can be encouraged by growing some flowers among your vegetables. Having a small wildflower garden too (see p. 72) will help the balance of nature to be tipped in your favour by providing a breeding ground for predators while shrubs and, of course, a bird table will encourage tits and other insect-feeding birds to visit your garden. Once they have been attracted by food scraps, they will happily turn their attention to living lunches.

Picking off affected leaves or other plant parts before diseases can spread is also often beneficial – the earliest signs of mildew on the tips of apple shoots in the spring for instance should be nipped off promptly. And of course with many pests such as slugs and caterpillars you can pick them off by hand (wearing a glove if you prefer). Although it obviously isn't practical to pick off individually very small pests such as aphids, the whole infested shoot tip – insects and all – can be pinched out where a small colony is established. (Broad beans are the classic examples of this.)

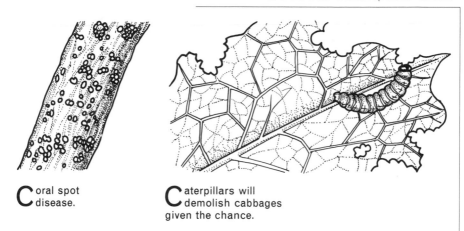

Coral spot disease.

Caterpillars will demolish cabbages given the chance.

In some instances, it simply isn't feasible to pinch out an aphid colony without losing a large part of your plant. A spray may then be your only recourse. But the spray that I suggest you use first is water. You can do a great deal of good simply by hosing or washing greenfly off a plant. You will need to repeat the treatment of course as some insects crawl back up and others fly in; but a hand sprayer full of tap water won't cost you very much. I should add that, strictly speaking, it is illegal to use any chemical which hasn't been officially approved for the purpose of controlling a pest – and water hasn't been officially approved. But I think that if you said that you were only washing your plants, and that the aphids were accidentally caught in the way, no one would mind.

Individual types of pest give rise to individual approaches to control. In greenhouses whiteflies and other pests can often be kept in check by hanging specially made inexpensive sticky yellow card strips among the plants (see p. 64). Slugs can be combatted at minimal cost with traps made from dishes sunk to their rims and filled with beer – the creatures crawl in and drown intoxicated. Spiny twigs placed around valuable beds of lettuces or other plants will also protect them from slugs and snails. With a bit of probing you will soon find that experienced gardening friends are full of cost-free homespun wisdom in garden pest control.

If all else fails and I really do have to resort to a proprietary spray, I try to follow the maxim of using a spray that I am sure is safe. And I think the safest general proprietary chemical insecticides are those based on natural soaps while the safest fungicides are those based on sulphur. Sadly, the safest soap-based sprays aren't the cheapest – which for the budget gardener underlines the importance of applying them only when absolutely necessary. Use general sprays, even soap-based ones, late in the evening when bees are likely to be in their hives. If aphids are your main problem an alternative to a general spray is to use the synthetic pesticide

JULY

pirimicarb. This will leave all of the beneficial insects unharmed and only kills aphids. It is also available combined successfully with a fungicide.

❀ **'BUDGET TIP'** A cost-saving approach to chemicals – is to apply one that does two jobs in one, controlling both pests and diseases.

TAKING CUTTINGS — THE HOME NURSERY

Nowhere in gardening is the expression 'something for nothing' as appropriate as in the subject of propagating plants from cuttings. From one plant you can make many more plants without tying up very much of your time. The plant may be a single individual that you have bought, one that is already growing in your garden, or one belonging to a friend who simply wishes you to share it. Cuttings can be taken at all times of the year but late summer is perhaps the busiest period.

A cutting is simply a piece cut from one plant and placed in soil or compost in conditions that will enable it to grow roots and so develop into a new plant. Usually the cutting is taken from the stem but, with some plants, leaves and roots too can be induced to produce new plants – or 'strike' – as gardeners call it.

Left: pelargoniums are very easy to root from softwood cuttings. Remove a length of shoot and trim it neatly to about 7.5 (3 in) below a leaf joint.
Right: snap off the lower leaves; they will simply rot if left.

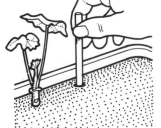
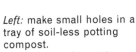
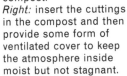
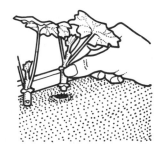

Left: make small holes in a tray of soil-less potting compost.
Right: insert the cuttings in the compost and then provide some form of ventilated cover to keep the atmosphere inside moist but not stagnant.

TYPES OF CUTTING Let's briefly look at the main different types of cutting and the times when they can be taken. Softwood cuttings are usually taken in the spring and early summer, usually from herbaceous or tender

JULY

perennials. As their name suggests the stem tissues are soft at that time and the cuttings fairly fragile. Piping cuttings are similar (see p. 75). As summer wears on the tissues toughen to become semi-ripe – as you bend them between finger and thumb, they are slightly springy. Many common garden shrubs can be propagated from semi-ripe cuttings. In winter, it is time to take hardwood cuttings, which are lengths of well matured stem, either leafless with deciduous plants, or still bearing foliage with evergreens.

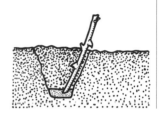

Roses are ideal subjects for hardwood cuttings. Trim a ripe shoot in late autumn to about 20–25 cm (8–10 in).

Remove the lower leaves – but be careful of the thorns.

Insert the cutting to two-thirds of its depth in a slit trench in a shady part of the garden, preferably with a little sand in the base of the trench.

HARDWOOD CUTTINGS Hardwood cuttings are the easiest to take. With pruners simply cut a portion of stem 20–25 cm (8–10 in) long just above and below buds. Carefully trim away any side shoots and insert it for two-thirds of its length in the soil in a shaded corner of the garden – or in a shaded cold frame if you have one.

Some plants commonly propagated from cuttings

Softwood cuttings	Semi-ripe cuttings	Hardwood cuttings
Carnations and pinks	Ceanothus	Buddleias
Dahlias	Potentillas	Dogwood
Delphiniums	Rhododendrons	Roses
Fuchsias	Rosemary	Weigela
Pelargoniums		Willows

Do be sure that you position the cutting with the growth buds facing upwards. Most types of hardwood cutting should root within 12 months and can then be dug up and replanted where you choose.

SEMI-RIPE AND SOFTWOOD CUTTINGS Semi-ripe and softwood cuttings need a little more protection for they will have leaves through which water can be lost and, until such time as they have new roots, they will be unable to replace the lost moisture. The answer is to place them not in the open ground but in some form of propagator. This sounds very grand but can

JULY

be as simple and inexpensive as a margarine pot with a plastic bag over the top held in place with a rubber band. The cover – be it plastic bag or something more sophisticated – is the important part for it maintains a saturated atmosphere around the plant and so limits water loss from the leaves. Semi-ripe or softwood cuttings are shorter than those of hardwood types – about 10–15 cm (4–6 in) long is usual. Try and take them from non-flowering shoots although, if flowers are present, they should be cut off. Trim or pull away the lower leaves so that the part of the stem to be inserted in the soil is bare of foliage. It will otherwise decay and the rot then spread to the entire cutting.

You can be certain that your cutting has produced roots and 'struck' successfully when there is elongation and new shoot growth and the cutting offers slight resistance when you 'nudge' it with your hand. But don't then be in too much of a hurry. Allow a further couple of weeks growth with the propagator cover at least partly off to allow ventilation and prevent mould growth. Then carefully move your new, and of course free plant to a pot of its own. Once it is growing well there it can be planted out in the garden after hardening off (see p. 17).

WILDFLOWERS IN YOUR GARDEN

Nothing has caught gardeners' imagination in recent years as much as wildlife gardening. Its appeal is considerable – wild plants are especially effective at encouraging beneficial insects to help control your pest problems, they will beautify your garden with their own flowers and by the butterflies that many will attract. And, carefully managed, they will provide a self-perpetuating feature that will cost you nothing in replanting costs each year.

But do remember that a wildflower garden is not just a patch of your garden that you have neglected. That would simply be a wilderness of rampant weeds, of neither use nor ornament.

To prepare a small wildflower 'meadow', you should dig the area as thoroughly as you would for any other type of garden, taking special care to clear any rampant perennial weeds (see p. 36) that will simply swamp your chosen plants. Above all, however, wildflower gardening has one important (and cost-saving) feature – absolutely no fertilizer should be used as this encourages lush grasses and leafy plants at the expense of attractive flowering types.

PLANTING A WILDFLOWER 'MEADOW' Buy a packet of wildflower meadow seed mixture and sow this as directed on the packet. This will give you a basic, grassy meadow with some wildflowers. But I have never found this on its own to be sufficient and you should also buy a few packets of selected chosen wildflowers to raise separately. Ox-eye daisy, ragged robin, scabious, corn cockle, corn chamomile, knapweed and teasel are all good as they will encourage a good range of butterflies, which will beautify your garden.

These individual plant species should be sown and raised in pots in the usual way (see p. 26) although you will find germination rather slower and more erratic than you may be used to with cultivated plants. Grow these in the pots for a year to give good-sized, strong individuals, which can then be planted out among the others in your 'meadow'.

Around late July, you will need to cut the meadow, much as farmers do, and allow the mowings to lie and dry on the ground, turning them several times with a fork. The 'hay' can be taken away and put on the compost heap.

❁ **'BUDGET TIP'** To avoid having to spend money on annual wildflower seeds each year and precious time sowing them, allow the mowings from the wildflower meadow to dry out. The seeds they contain can then mature and be shed so that the annual species will be replenished for next year.

OTHER PLANTS THAT ATTRACT BUTTERFLIES Finally, a few inexpensive and easy to grow cultivated species can also be guaranteed to bring butterflies into your budget garden:
● Butterfly bush (*Buddleia davidii*) (*below*) in its purple, blue, red or white flowered varieties (all are lovely);
● Low-growing, late summer flowering, herbaceous, perennial ice plant (*Sedum spectabile*);
● Michaelmas daisies; and
● Orange-flowered bedding tagetes, which I find is so much better than its much larger-flowered, more showy relatives – the African and French marigolds.

JOBS FOR JULY

GENERAL

You will learn a great deal about gardening through the guidance and inspiration of the experts. Therefore don't miss any of your favourite radio and television programmes – their information comes for nothing more than the cost of your licence fee.

JULY

THE INDOOR GARDEN

Thinking of holidays again, and concerned that all of your precious plants should fry if there is a hot spell whilst you are away, may I suggest that you move them. Group them together in the coolest room of the house (provided it is reasonably well lit) and stand them in dishes of water.

CONTAINERS

Continue to water and feed plants of all types in containers. Take special care with growing bags for the compost can so easily dry out unseen.

If you are planning to go away on holiday, do try to make arrangements for a neighbour to help with watering. Hanging baskets are the most vulnerable to drying out but I find the best solution is to lift them down and stand them on a wide bowl of water in a shady place. Any plants that emerge directly from the underside of the basket will suffer rather, but the basket as a whole should come through unscathed.

GREENHOUSES, COLD FRAMES AND CLOCHES

If the weather is very hot, leave the greenhouse door open all through July. At this time of year the temperature never drops low enough to cause any harm and you will certainly prevent your plants from being cooked.

Once your tomato plants have produced five trusses (fruit clusters), pinch out the top of the plants. Continue to pinch out any new growth at the top to avoid reducing the quality of your crop by weakening the plants. Continue to give liquid feed twice a week.

Look carefully for any signs of red spider mite. This pest produces very fine webbing on indoor plants of all kinds, the leaves become bronzed and eventually may wither. It is very difficult to control but misting regularly with plain water will certainly help.

LAWN

Mysterious brown patches can appear on the lawn at this time of year. The commonest culprits are bitches but leatherjacket larvae in the soil are the next most probable cause. You can diminish their numbers significantly by watering the affected patch in the evening and then laying old plastic bags or sheet over the surface, weighted down at the edges. Lift them in the morning, when the larvae will have come to the surface. They can then be swept up and put in a dish on the bird table.

❀ **'BUDGET TIP'** It is a false economy to use fresh lawn mowings as a mulch on beds and borders. They can become very hot and will temporarily decrease the amount of nitrogen plant food in the soil. They should always be composted before use as a mulch.

THE FLOWER GARDEN

JULY

Continue to dead-head perennials and annuals alike as the summer wears on.

❀ **'BUDGET TIP'** Home-made pot pourri is rather special – and makes a good, cheap present too. So why not mix your own? Essential ingredients are rose petals and lavender, both of which can be collected now. But don't make the mistake of waiting until the flowers have faded on lavender. Clip them just as the flowers become fully open.

Sweet peas are prone to infestation by the black pollen beetles which spread into gardens from oil seed rape crops. Unfortunately, it is all but impossible to control so don't waste time and money trying to spray.

❀ **'BUDGET TIP'** Nasturtiums are doubly valuable this month: their edible flowers make very colour additions to summer salads, as well as looking marvellous in a vase.

Pinks and carnations make lovely additions to the garden but, unfortunately, tend to become straggly after a few years unless they are renewed. Now is the time to do this most cost-effectively by taking the easiest of cuttings called pipings. Just pull out the ends of some non-flowering shoots, which will come away, telescope fashion. Then push them into sandy compost in a simple propagator (see p. 27).

VEGETABLES

The results of your labours really begin to be apparent this month but it's a shame to spoil your plants at the very moment of harvesting. Take care especially when picking peas and beans as you can easily uproot the plants and so lose them. Use two hands to pick pea pods and a small pair of scissors or snips to pick runner beans.

Don't imagine that salads will finish with the summer. At the end of July sow some winter lettuce, curly endive and winter radish. With the help of a little protection from cloches, you can have free, fresh salads when they are very pricey in the shops.

If you have a frost-free greenhouse, then plant a few potato tubers this month in a large container. A big bucket or old dustbin is ideal. Fill it with garden soil and some garden compost plus a handful of fertilizer. With luck, you will have at least some home-grown potatoes to serve with the turkey at Christmas.

Look out for the male flowers on courgette plants. These are the blooms with no small swelling behind them. They should be pulled off so that all of the plant's energies can be directed towards the female, fruit-bearing

JULY

flowers. First, dab the male flowers into the females however in order to help pollination.

Keep using the hoe to weed between your crops whenever the weather is dry – but never hoe close to onions as you could damage them by disturbing their shallow roots.

FRUIT

Once your strawberries have cropped for three years, they will require replacement.

❀ **'BUDGET TIP'** Strawberry runners will be developing in July and these are your means of obtaining new plants for nothing. Peg down some of the runners and then, when they have rooted, sever them from the parent plant, and pot them up for replanting in a new bed.

Once the fruit has been picked from raspberry plants, the old fruited canes are useless to the plant and should be cut back to soil level, so that the plant can concentrate its energy in preparing for next year's crop.

If you are growing any of your fruit plants as cordons, they will need pruning around the middle of July.

TREES AND SHRUBS

July is the month when a great deal of hedge-cutting is done because bird nesting is now well out of the way and so they won't be disturbed. Keep standing back from the hedge as you clip it. Otherwise, you could easily find yourself clipping a hole. And unless you have a very good eye, you will find it worthwhile stretching a straight, taut string along the side to show you where to cut.

Variegated trees and shrubs can be very attractive but some of them are prone to 'revert' and produce plain green shoots which are more vigorous. Cut these shoots out before they take over the entire plant.

Do be sure that young trees and shrubs aren't being crowded out by grass or weed growth around the base. They should have a clear area of soil around the base of the main stem.

CLIMBERS

By the end of July, wisterias should have had their first pruning of the year in order to encourage a better show of flowers. Once the main framework of the plant is established against your wall, all of the long, whippy shoots should be cut back to about 25 cm (10 in) from the base.

HOT AND CHANGEABLE

PLANT OF THE MONTH FOR AUGUST

Fuchsia 'Genii' (Fuchsia)

IT'S CERTAINLY UNARGUABLE that fuchsias flower for longer than most small shrubs and therefore are a great asset to the budget gardener. Amongst them, there are some gems, especially when you turn to the species and near species. In choosing one, I was torn between the pendulous, red-flowered, half-hardy 'Thalia', which can be brought indoors in autumn, and my final selection – a hardy variety which has the unusual attribute of yellow foliage. It might be thought that its small purple and red flowers together with yellow leaves would be a bilious combination but somehow it works well. The plants will reach a height of about 45–60 cm (18–24 in) and should be cut down in spring, having had the dead stems left on overwinter for protection. Some compost mounded around the crowns will also help to prevent frost from penetrating.

J	F	M	A	M	J	J	A	S	O	N	D
						F	F	F	F		
				L		L	L	L	L	L	

F flowers, L leaves, Fr fruit, S stems [ ] denotes in some years

WATERING

There is a new hardy perennial that makes its presence felt at about this time every year. It's called drought and I'm sure that there is no aspect of gardening in which the notion of saving has become more evident or more important in recent years than the subject of water. In the British Isles there is now a national water shortage, one that just won't go away, and most people also appreciate that water costs money. I suppose this is most evident if your water supply is metered but, even for those of us still receiving a bill twice a year, the price increases have been very

AUGUST

noticeable. When water costs were simply part of the rates, we all took it pretty much for granted.

COPING WITH DROUGHT The consequences for gardeners are especially important because around 90 per cent of the bulk of any plant is water – which must come from somewhere. I find there are several ways to approach the business of cost and resource saving:
● Use as much as possible of free natural water (rain to you and me);
● Re-use some of your domestic water (the water you have already paid for);
● Apply all and any water to your plants in the most efficient way possible; and
● Grow the types of plant that are more drought tolerant.

All rain that falls on to the soil will of course drain away sooner or later; the trick is to make it later. And you can do this by improving the water-holding, 'sponge-like' properties of your garden soil by digging in and mulching with as much compost and other organic matter as possible. I've talked elsewhere about the value of organic matter for improving soil structure (see p. 9) and the economic importance of mulching for weed control (see p. 88), yet the effects on moisture retentiveness can be pretty dramatic too. In a long-term experiment in a vegetable garden, compost was dug in at the rate of 6 kg per sq. m (1.23 lb per sq. ft) over a period of years and it increased the amount of water available to the plants by 50 per cent. But in many areas, especially in the drier, eastern part of Britain, rainfall is itself too erratic to ensure that your plants receive sufficient water during the summer months. This is where catching and storing the rain is important.

SAVING RAIN WATER A rain-water butt is one of the best water-saving investments you can make. Butts come in different sizes and the cost works out at about £0.22 per lit. (£1 per gal.) of storage capacity – a 114 lit. (25 gal.) butt costs about £25 and so on.

❀ 'BUDGET TIP' Don't try to economize by buying a slightly cheaper model with no lid and no tap. The lid keeps out algae and fungal spores that would soon foul the water and ruin your plants; and a tap near the bottom is essential if you actually want to take water out of the thing.

Position the rain-water butt close to the down-pipe from the guttering on your house or on an outbuilding if you have one.

Most of the domestic water that runs down the drain after you have used it can be put to secondary use in the garden.

❀ **'BUDGET TIP'** A cost-effective way to water your garden plants with domestic water is by diverting the down-pipe drain from your bath to a water butt or other collection tank and taking it to your garden from there. The average bath contains 80 lit. (18 gal.) of water, sufficient to supply all of the water needed for 3 sq. m (32 sq. ft) of vegetable garden for the whole summer.

Water that contains normal soap and washing up liquid is perfectly safe for all except very young seedlings. But do avoid using any water with bleach or other chemical additives – and I'm pretty sure that dishwater soaps are a bit too vicious for plant life.

Perhaps I should just add that whilst everyone agrees that water must be used as efficiently as possible, in times of severe drought some water companies have been concerned at their sewage plants not working properly because everyone is putting waste water on their gardens. Do check locally if you are in doubt about what is permissible.

WATERING METHODS Bear in mind too that most garden water is wasted in the way it is used. Unattended sprinklers attached to hosepipes are the biggest culprits. They can use as much as 1 tonne (1 ton) of water in an hour; and a large proportion of it, especially in the kitchen garden, will fall on the bare soil between your plants rather than around their roots. A hand-held hose is a great deal more accurate because you can place the water close to the plants, just where it is needed. And of course a watering can (essential if you have a hosepipe ban) is more accurate still.

Incidentally, if you do wish to use a hose and/or a sprinkler, do check first with your local water company for they differ in their need and may charge for a permit. And the fact that a permit could itself cost you a fee is yet another reason for a budget gardener not to use a sprinkler. In any event never water your lawn unless it is a newly sown one; you will need vast quantities of water to make any significant difference to its appearance and lawn turf is extremely durable and will always recover after a drought.

WHEN TO WATER Lawns aside, all other garden plants should be watered efficiently – that is the water should be given at the time when they will most benefit from it. My rule of thumb for this is to water when the object of growing the plant is coming to fruition. So water:
● Flowers as the flower buds begin to swell and open;
● Fruit bushes as the fruit are swelling and ripening;
● Lettuces as the hearts begin to fill; and
● Peas and beans as the flowers set and the pods start to fill.

It's obviously a bit harder to see what is happening under the soil, but for potatoes, the key is to wait until the flowers form as this indicates that the tubers are starting to swell.

Plants growing in containers need more than usual attention to watering for they have no reserves to tap at depth in the soil. And hanging baskets are the containers most in need of attention – they really must be watered once a day and so make little sense for someone with very limited amounts of water to use, or not much time to spare.

An inverted plastic bottle with the bottom cut off makes a good irrigator.

African daisies (Cape Marigolds).

DROUGHT-TOLERANT PLANTS Wherever possible choose plants that are drought tolerant, especially if you know that you will be away from home a good deal and unable to tend to them as often as you might wish. In general plants with large, thin leaves need a great deal of water; those with tough, more fleshy leaves rather less. Among ornamentals, plants with grey, silvery or slightly woolly foliage, along with many prickly plants and many herbs, originate naturally in warm, dry areas with a Mediterranean type of climate and these are excellent at surviving without water for long periods. Many of our most popular garden annual flowers such as pelargoniums and African daisies come originally from South Africa and I always find this is a good indication of drought tolerance – the notes on the seed packet or in the catalogue will often tell you the origin of plants.

SAVING YOUR OWN SEEDS

I happen to think that a packet of seeds still represents some of the best value in gardening but, even here, costs are creeping up year by year and a season's seed bill can come to several pounds. Yet in August there are seeds in large quantities just asking to be used for nothing. These are the seeds that are produced on your own garden plants and it is wasteful not

AUGUST

to make good use of them. It's unadventurous too, because sometimes an interesting new flower colour variation or shape may arise among some of your home-produced seedlings.

WHICH SEEDS TO SAVE It is worth saving seed from most but not quite all types of plant, because some ornamentals – most notably those with double flowers – produce almost no seeds at all and are always propagated by cuttings. The most important plants to avoid, both among vegetables and flowers, are the F1 hybrid varieties. Your original seed packet will tell you which these are. Seeds from F1 hybrids produce a useless hotch-potch of seedlings, which do not share many of the characteristics of their parents. Each year, therefore, seed companies have to make afresh the original crosses to produce F1 hybrid seeds. A wise and thrifty gardener, however, is likely to have only few F1 hybrid seeds as they are always the most expensive – reflecting the labour intensive way in which they are produced.

The trick with collecting seeds is to act in good time – before they are shed naturally and fall on to the ground. Slip a paper (*not* plastic) bag over the seed head and tie it firmly around the stem to collect the seeds as they drop. Once you have a good catch, cut off the stem, open the bag and allow the seeds to dry for a few days at room temperature. They can then be put in old envelopes, secured with a paper clip, labelled and stored in the usual way (see p. 28).

❋ **'BUDGET TIP'** A cellophane bag slipped over a seed head is a labour saving and ideal way to collect seed because you can see at a glance exactly what is happening to the head inside.

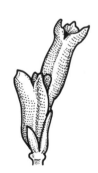

Removing seeds from a dry seed head.

A HERB GARDEN

Summer in my garden is always enhanced by the delicious aroma of fresh herbs and you too can benefit financially by growing your own herbs. I was astonished recently see just how the cost of fresh herbs has rocketed in supermarkets. For the price of the smallest bunch of parsley, you could buy enough seeds for a garden full. All of the herbs that you see in the shops can be grown in your own garden, and almost all can also be grown

AUGUST

in pots on a window-sill. (Generally spices are different, however, for they are produced from tropical plants and can't be grown at home).

TYPES OF HERB There are essentially two main types of herb: perennials and annuals. The majority are perennials such as thyme, sage, marjoram and tarragon. Most will grow well for about four or five years before they need dividing or renewing from cuttings or new plants.

Some herbs can be raised annually from seed: parsley (which is fully hardy) and basil (which isn't) are the commonest of these. You may be slightly confused by seed packets of most of the perennial types too. There's no denying that thyme, sage and the rest can be grown from seed – although they aren't always particularly easy to germinate – but I see no merit in it. The varieties of these herbs that can be seed-raised are almost invariably not as well-flavoured as those that are bought as plants – 'Silver Posie' for example is a delicious thyme variety and 'Apple Mint' the best-flavoured mint.

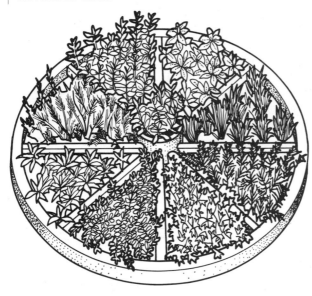

An old cartwheel (or even a home-made copy) makes a spectacular pretty herb garden. Between the spokes of the wheel, you can grow such easy and traditional herbs as thymes, sages, mint, marjoram, chives and parsley.

❀ **'BUDGET TIP'** If you want only one plant of thyme, it's cheaper to buy that one plant than to raise seedlings – bearing in mind not only the cost of your time but also that of the seed packet and seed compost.

GROWING HERBS A small herb garden will occupy only a couple of square metres or yards and should be positioned, if at all possible, close to the kitchen door, where it really will be used. Most herbs require a fairly light, free-draining soil, just a little fertilizer at the beginning of the season and are good at surviving periods of drought. The perennial types can be lightly trimmed back after flowering but in general they need very little attention. The only herb likely to become at all mischievous is mint, which can be remarkably invasive.

❀ **'BUDGET TIP'** To escape the time-consuming task of keeping invasive mint in check, grow it in a large plastic pot or an old bucket, sunk to its rim in the soil. Lift the container each autumn and trim off any roots and runners that are threatening to escape.

JOBS FOR AUGUST

GENERAL

Compost is best made most economically by turning the heap or contents of the compost bin at least once, ensuring that the material on the outside is brought to the centre to heat through. August is a good time of year to do it, when the heat loss to the atmosphere is minimal.

THE INDOOR GARDEN

Any necessary re-potting should be completed by the end of this month (see p. 31).

❀ **'BUDGET TIP'** Keep a look-out for reductions in the price of house plants. In August DIY stores and supermarkets may well be clearing shelf space to make way for autumn goods and be selling off plants of all types very cheaply.

CONTAINERS

Towards the end of the month, plants in hanging baskets will be looking rather jaded. Dead-heading, removing old leaves and feeding can help to prolong their lives but there comes a point when it is better to cut your losses and replant the baskets with fresh compost for winter.

❀ **'BUDGET TIP'** A free and rather special way to fill up evergreen winter baskets is simply by walking around the garden and collecting self-sown ivies, little conifers and other seedlings.

GREENHOUSES, COLD FRAMES AND CLOCHES

❀ **'BUDGET TIP'** To get optimum value from your tomato crop keep feeding them to prolong the cropping period for as long as possible. And continue to pinch out side-shoots and tie in the stems.

On a warm dry day wash all of the pots and seed trays that you never found time to deal with in the spring. It's important that they will be clean ready for next season's seedlings and at this time of year, you should have ample opportunity to do it whilst the weather is warm and sunny enough for them to dry outside.

If you want to have your own hyacinths for Christmas – either for the house or as a gift – you will need specially treated bulbs, which are on sale now. These should be planted around the end of the month. For the best effect, choose varieties of the same colour as these will tend to grow at the same rate. Pot the bulbs up separately in small individual pots (so if one dies and rots, it will not harm the others).

❀ **'BUDGET TIP' Rather than buying special-purpose bulb compost save money by re-using fairly dry old soil-less potting compost for your container-grown bulbs.**

Wrap the pots in newspaper and bury them in a cool spot in the garden. They will need to be checked for shoot development in about eight weeks, when they can slowly be brought into a cool room of the house. Group together individual pots containing plants of similar size and then, finally, when the flower spike develops, bring them into full warmth.

LAWN

If you have some lawn weedkiller (see p. 37), make up a small amount in an old watering can (one that won't be used for watering or feeding plants) to spot-treat lawn weeds. Alternatively, make up the mixture in a bucket and use a small scoop to apply it to individual weed clumps. This is very much more economical than watering over the whole lawn. But only apply the weedkiller when the soil is already moist after a heavy summer shower. After use, all waste garden chemicals, diluted or not, should be washed with plenty of water down an outside drain.

If you didn't manage to sow or lay your new lawn in the spring, autumn is the next best time. At the end of August therefore, you should begin to prepare the soil, taking special care to remove any perennial weeds.

THE FLOWER GARDEN

We all find that to make the most of our gardens, we need to move some plants in the beds and borders in the autumn. But will you then be able to remember where each type grew and which colour each variety had? In my experience, the answer is 'no'. So make a few notes now of things that will need re-arrangement once they have died down for the season.

This is the best month to take cuttings from pelargoniums. There is no plant that can be multiplied so easily and simply but I must offer a word of warning. There is no point in taking cuttings now if you don't have the space to store them frost-free overwinter – bear in mind that they will take up a fair amount of room.

❧ **'BUDGET TIP'** If your storage space is limited, a cost-effective and practical way to multiply your pelargonium stock is to store a few plants over the winter and take the cuttings instead in the spring.

Clear away plants from the flower garden as and when they obviously begin to fade. It will be much easier to chop them for composting a few at a time, rather than find that you have a mass of material to contend with all at once.

Too many gardeners think of bulbs for spring alone but there are many delightful, autumn-flowering species such as colchicum and autumn crocus. These bulbs will now be in the shops and, if you time it correctly, you should be able to obtain some at reduced prices as soon as the mass of spring-flowering bulbs comes in to take their place.

A second crop of weeds often tends to emerge at about this time of year – just as the mulch that you put on in spring is finally breaking down. Choose a dry day and use your hoe to chop them down.

VEGETABLES

Dig potatoes carefully so as not to spear them. Always pick up even the tiniest potatoes, which will be of no use for eating but, if you leave them, the chances are that they will grow next year and the resulting plants will be a nuisance among the crops that you are growing in that plot next season.

❧ **'BUDGET TIP'** It's important to obtain the maximum yield from all of your crops. So keep runner beans well watered in order to assist the flower trusses to set and form pods.

As soon as you have some free areas in the kitchen garden plant out the winter lettuce that you sowed in July. The sooner it is established the better, and then in autumn you will have good strong plants over which you can place cloches.

Sow a few rows of 'Winter Hardy White Lisbon' spring onions. They will grow slowly over the winter and be ready for harvesting next spring. But do be sure to use the winter hardy variant, not just plain 'White Lisbon'. The longer you are able to keep your soil filled with plants, the better will be the value you obtain from your garden.

If you have grown bulb onions, now is the time to harvest them, but do allow the bulbs to lie on the surface of the soil for a few days to ripen fully before you store them in nets.

AUGUST

FRUIT

Don't try to economize by storing the earliest varieties of apples (those that mature this month). These should be eaten fresh and only the later varieties used for keeping.

❀ **'BUDGET TIP'** To obtain the best value from your apples use them imaginatively. For example if you have only one tree and only one variety, why not swap bags of apples with neighbours who have other types? In this way everyone has a share of the earlies, later varieties, eaters and cookers.

The wood of plums and damsons is very brittle and on old trees, you can lose both a fair proportion of your maturing crop and a large part of the plant when branches snap under the weight. Over the years, I have come to appreciate that a wooden prop is essential on wide-spreading branches of old trees.

❀ **'BUDGET TIP'** Why not make more economical use of your apples by cooking them with blackberries? If you don't have blackberries in your garden, then the fruit ripening on wild hedgerow plants by the end of August will be tempting. Strictly you should ask farmers or other owners if you may pick them, although most won't mind provided you don't stray from footpaths. But never pick fruit from along petrol-contaminated roadsides.

TREES AND SHRUBS

Continue to dead-head roses through the summer in order to obtain a regular supply of new blooms. And repeat your sprays against aphids and diseases as necessary.

❀ **'BUDGET TIP'** A free way to increase or renew your stock is to take hardwood cuttings (see p. 71) from ornamental shrubs (including roses) at the end of August. You could swap the new plants with friends.

If you have trees or shrubs that are becoming rather too large for their positions, now is the time to cut out large branches that are misplaced or making the plant top-heavy.

CLIMBERS

Take cuttings from clematis (see p. 70). Unlike most other plants, clematis cuttings are best cut between rather than just below, the nodes (the swellings from which the leaf clusters arise) and pushed into the compost up to the level of the node. You will have the best success from the species such as *Clematis montana* or *C. tangutica*; some of the large flowered hybrids such as 'Nellie Moser' aren't as easy.

Prune wisterias by cutting the long, whippy green shoots back to 20 cm (10 in).

THE HARVEST RIPENS

PLANT OF THE MONTH FOR SEPTEMBER

Sorbus **'Joseph Rock'**

THIS DECIDUOUS TREE with its rich autumn leaf colours, white, foamy blossom in late spring and delightful yellow berries in late summer and early autumn is an ideal choice for the budget garden. It provides an interesting contrast to the normal, red berried mountain ash. There are several species and hybrids related to the wild rowan tree, but in my experience this is the best of those that are readily obtainable. It is fairly slow-growing and will reach about 6 m (20 ft) after 15 years so, whilst not a tree for a tiny garden, it is excellent for a medium-sized one. 'Joseph Rock' is easily grown in almost any type of soil, and is generally free from pests and diseases although the leaves may be slightly affected by nibbling insects in summer. Its relatively long, clear trunk is excellent for surrounding with bulbs and clump-forming herbaceous perennials.

J	F	M	A	M	J	J	A	S	O	N	D
			L	F	F	L	FR	FR	FR	FR	
							L	L	L	L	

F flowers, L leaves, Fr fruit, S stems [ ] denotes in some years

---

MAKING COMPOST

For me, making and using compost embodies everything about money saving, sound gardening practice. Not to make use of as much organic debris as possible is not only stupidly wasteful of money, but is also almost criminally wasteful of a valuable natural resource. And as autumn approaches this organic debris is available in its most abundant quantities. If you don't have a compost bin already, now is the moment to make one.

I hope it will be apparent already that I place greater store by using organic matter in the garden than almost anything else. Dug into the

SEPTEMBER

garden it is the key to good soil, which itself is the key to good gardening. It also provides some plant food and, used as a mulch, is invaluable in helping to suppress weed growth and retain moisture. In all respects, making and using compost will save you money and time as no other gardening operation can.

SUITABLE MATERIALS First, however, let's consider which materials can and should be composted, and which are the very few that shouldn't:

● Pretty well all plant remains from the garden or the kitchen may be used, including weeds. Good composting, done as I suggest (see below) will kill all weed seeds. The only exceptions to this general advice are couch grass rhizomes, which ought to be decomposed during good composting although the risk of any escaping is too great to take, and any plant remains that are infected with one of two diseases: clubroot and whiterot. Clubroot causes swelling on the roots of plants in the cabbage family whereas whiterot causes fluffy, white mould on the bulbs of onions (spring onions especially). Both are almost impossible to eradicate from garden soil and will probably survive the composting process. It just isn't worth the risk of spreading them therefore and so they should be bagged up for the municipal tip.

● Woody material is very good for composting as it helps to balance the softer matter such as lawn mowings. The difficulty is in breaking it down first into small enough pieces. In a small garden modest piles of prunings can be chopped up with secateurs but larger quantities really are impractical. If you have a good rotary lawnmower you can chop up small, twiggy material by spreading it on the grass and running the mower over it.

● Leaves of course are good and organic and must be made use of – there will be thousands of them to deal with over the next few weeks. Because they tend to break down more slowly than other organic matter, however, they can block a compost bin and prevent the free flow of air and water through it. For this reason they are much better raked together (use your spring tine rake to collect them and then two pieces of board to pick them up) and stacked separately in a cage (see p. 90) to make leaf mould for mulching.

● All domestic organic waste can be composted with the exception of animal products such as chicken carcasses which may attract vermin. And of course, non-organic matter such as plastic and metal can't be used.

● Paper waste – here the composting operation can be counter-productive. Even though pretty well all paper is organic, glossy magazine paper never rots down very well. The problem with the remainder is that in sheet form, it acts in the same way as leaves and tends to block the flow of water and air into the compost; it really should be shredded. If you are prepared to tear all of your waste paper into thin strips therefore, do use it; otherwise it is better tied up and taken to the local recycling centre.

COMPOST BINS So much for the ingredients, now for the container. You will notice that I've talked of a compost *bin*, not a compost *heap*. The distinction is important for the secret of making compost properly is that it should heat up thoroughly and this is something that won't happen in a simple heap. You need a bin of some sort and whilst wood or plastic ones can be purchased, it is simplicity itself (and inexpensive) for anyone remotely handy to knock one together.

I have always found that compost needs some aeration and this is why, unlike some gardeners, I always use a bin with slatted rather than solid sides.

❀ **'BUDGET TIP'** As the most efficient bin size is about 1 m (39 in) cube, it can be made cheaply from four old wooden pallets, which are readily obtainable. Give the wood a thorough coating with preservative (I still think creosote is best), nail or screw three pallets together and then use a little ingenuity to reconstruct the fourth side such that it can be taken out, either plank by plank or half at a time for ease of access.

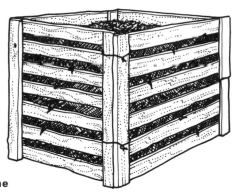

If you have a large garden, you will find a double bin is best – the contents of one can be decomposing whilst the other is being filled. A very small garden may require something smaller than 1 m (39 in) cube, in this case you will need to rebuild the pallets. Straightforward, old wooden planks may be simpler in such circumstances.

Try to blend the waste as you fill your compost bin – mix soft, green material with slightly tougher debris. For every 20 cm (8 in) or so of depth it is advisable to add a layer of a nitrogen source for the composting bacteria to work efficiently. Fresh manure is ideal if you have any; if not, then use a proprietary compost accelerator. (The best known brand, Garotta, costs about £2.50 for a 1.5 kg (3.3 lb) pack which will last a couple of years.) Contrary to common belief there is no need to add soil.

❀ **'BUDGET TIP'** Even cheaper than a proprietary compost accelerator is sulphate of ammonia, which costs only half as much.

Compost shouldn't be allowed to dry out but nor should it become soggy. In dry weather you may need to pour a can or two of water on top

SEPTEMBER

once a week whilst in winter, especially if the bin is fully exposed in the open, a layer of old sacking, carpet or similar material on top will help keep off the worst of the rain. Usually compost will be ready for use in about six months.

LEAF MOULD CAGE A leaf mould cage can be made even more cost-effectively and simply than a compost bin. The dimensions should be roughly the same, about 1 m (39 in) cube with four stout wooden corner posts and some old chicken wire (the smaller the mesh, the better) wrapped around them. Leaves compress to many times less than their original volume and so as you fill the cage, you (or your children) will find it useful to jump on them. Leaf mould should be ready for spreading as mulch in about 12 months.

MULTIPLYING YOUR PLANTS BY DIVISION

Seed sowing and taking cuttings are all part of obtaining more plants at little or no cost. But there is nothing in gardening that is more money-saving and easier than to increase the number of plants by dividing them into several pieces. It might at first sight seem to be a contradiction but you do actually end up with more. And autumn is the very best time to do this, followed by spring, especially for slightly more tender types.

Not all plants can be propagated in this way although it is possible with many of the most important. Almost all herbaceous perennials can be divided and when you realize that this group encompasses such familiar standbys as hardy geraniums, Michaelmas daisies, phlox, campanulas and hostas, you will appreciate its value. Primulas and numerous other small perennial rock garden plants also divide very satisfactorily. Although it can be achieved with especial care division is usually least successful with those types of perennial that have brittle or fleshy roots such as lupins and paeonies. With very few exceptions, shrubs and other woody plants can't be propagated by division although in modified form it can be done with many types of bulb (see p. 105).

THE DIVISION TECHNIQUE Division is simplicity itself. Dig up the plant, preferably with a fork, and pull the clump into several smaller pieces. If the clump is fairly small, as with primroses for example, much the best plan is to pull the whole apart with your hands but, with larger, tougher rootstocks use a combination of fork, spade, knife, boot and ingenuity. In essence, the plan is to tear rather than chop, for chopping is likely to damage the roots, make re-growth difficult and possibly admit decay fungi.

SEPTEMBER

U se tools to divide tough rootstocks.　　S maller plants can be divided by hand.

Although the result of division will be more plants at no cost, it also rejuvenates the plant and makes sure that it will give you many more years of value. Do be sure, therefore, not to replant all of the pieces – reject those that were originally towards the centre of the clump for they will be browned and moribund. Use only the fresh, vigorous parts towards the periphery. Almost all plants that are amenable to the technique should be divided at regular intervals – about once every four or five years is sufficient for most, although many types of primula in particular tend to deteriorate unless they are divided every two or three years.

USING SHRUBS FOR MAXIMUM EFFECT

The shrub is without doubt the best-value plant in any garden – best value that is in money terms for they will last almost forever and in terms of labour because they require relatively little effort on your part. There is a shrub for every garden and every situation. Flowering shrubs are available for every season while foliage shrubs occur with an amazing range of colour and leaf shape in both evergreen and deciduous species. Moreover in all of these groups there is a range of sizes from soil-hugging and weed-suppressing, ground-cover varieties to medium-sized types that blend with other shrubs and with herbaceous perennials, bulbs and annuals in beds and borders through to tall specimens that will create splendid isolated features.

❀ **'BUDGET TIP'** Save money by asking your friends or neighbours if you can take cuttings from their favourite shrubs instead of incurring the expense of buying a new shrub from a garden centre or nursery.

It is very difficult to draw up a short list from the thousands of shrub varieties available, but the dozen in the table are my personal suggestions

SEPTEMBER

Shrubs that offer good value for money

SHRUB	ULTIMATE HEIGHT (if correctly pruned)	FEATURES
*Aucuba japonica**	4 m (13 ft)	Variegated leaves, will grow in dry shade where almost nothing else will
Buddleia davidii (Butterfly bush)	3.5 m (11 ft 6 in)	Attracts butterflies; prune hard in early spring
Cotoneaster horizontalis (Wall-spray)	60 cm (2 ft)	Spreading ground cover with good, autumn berries
Euonymus fortunei 'Sunspot'*	60 cm (2 ft)	Very pretty, dark green foliage with yellow blotch
Jasminum nudiflorum (Winter jasmine)	3 m (10 ft)	Bright yellow flowers during the dullest part of the New Year; trim lightly in spring
Philadelphus 'Manteau d'Hermine'	75 cm (2 ft 6 in)	Delicious, white, double flowers in spring
Pieris 'Forest Flame'*	2 m (6 ft 6 in)	For acid soils, vivid red, young shoots
Potentilla	1.5 m (4 ft 6 in)	Most varieties have a very long summer-flowering period

SHRUB	ULTIMATE HEIGHT	FEATURES
Spiraea 'Arguta' (Bridal Wreath, Foam of May)	2 m (6 ft 6 in)	Delicate, white flowers in spring
Viburnum bodnantense	5 m (17 ft)	Very reliable for pretty pink, winter flowers
*Vinca minor** (Lesser periwinkle)	75 cm (2 ft 6 in)	Very pretty, blue-flowered ground cover for almost all soils
Weigela 'Florida Variegata'	2 m (6 ft 6 in)	White-margined leaves and pink flowers

* evergreen

of shrubs that offer especially good value for money for the budget gardener, being both inexpensive and notably effective in their particular role. Unless I have stated otherwise no special pruning is needed and the shrub is deciduous.

SHRUB CARE Some shrubs require pruning but most will grow satisfactorily for many years with little more than the periodic cutting away of old and worn out branches. Provided the planting position was well prepared with compost and bonemeal, a young shrub will establish quickly and reward you well with no further attention other than clearing away weeds from its base so nutrients are not diverted. The results will be even better however if you apply a handful of general fertilizer (see p. 45) in early spring.

JOBS FOR SEPTEMBER

GENERAL

Send away for seed catalogues which are usually issued during September. They make wonderfully inspirational reading and contain masses of free gardening information.

❀ **'BUDGET TIP'** Check whether any seed company is offering a bonus such as some free packets of seeds if you order before a certain date.

THE INDOOR GARDEN

Azaleas and other indoor plants that have been enjoying a summer holiday outdoors should now be brought in again. I always find that the signal for bringing them in is when you feel that you need to switch on your heating, at least at nights. But before you do bring your plants indoors do check the pots for worms, slugs and snails: finding them crawling across your carpet isn't the best welcome for your family and visitors.

CONTAINERS

By the end of the month, you will have to say goodbye to bedding plants in any tubs or other containers that you want to use for bulbs or for winter-flowering pansies.

❀ **'BUDGET TIP'** Don't waste good plants. Pelargoniums and fuchsias can be cut down and either potted up for keeping in a frost-free greenhouse or allowed to dry and wrapped in newspaper for storing in cardboard boxes in a shed or garage. Good specimens of other bedding plants can be tidied up and potted for use as house plants. Even if they only give you a display for a few weeks it will have been a cost-free bonus.

❀ **'BUDGET TIP'** Don't throw away the soil-less compost in old growing bags. It can be re-used one more time in various ways: bulb fibre (see p. 104); late annuals (see p. 94), and a medium in which to overwinter dahlias (see p. 31).

GREENHOUSES, COLD FRAMES AND CLOCHES

As with outdoor tomatoes at the end of August, so greenhouse crops will be reaching the end of their productive time now; and in any event will need to be removed to make way for other plants being overwintered.

SEPTEMBER

SEPTEMBER

Keep the green fruits for ripening (see p. 94).

Choose a warm day to clear the greenhouse and take out everything. If you have been keeping bubble film insulation on through the summer (see p. 19), this must also be removed. Then use a hand brush with a bucket of hot soapy water to clean down the whole of the inside structure. Finally rinse it with clean water and allow it to dry off and then replace the insulation.

From the end of this month, any plants being kept in the greenhouse will need watering very little – once a week should be ample.

Cloches should be in place by the end of September on plants being grown outdoors for winter use. If you have glass cloches, be sure that the glass is clean before using them as dirt will cut down light transmission very considerably.

LAWN

In September new lawns may be laid and old ones reseeded or returfed (see p. 47). Unless you have some special proprietary autumn feed stop feeding your lawn to prevent soft lush growth, prone to damage in the winter.

THE FLOWER GARDEN

By the end of September, many areas will have experienced their first frosts. This will mark the end of another season for the tender perennials, especially dahlias and gladioli. As soon as dahlia foliage has blackened, lift the tubers, cut down the stems to about 10 cm (4 in) and stand the clumps upside down to dry. Then gently poke out any soil from between the tubers and store them in almost dry, old, soil-less compost in boxes somewhere frost-free.

Gladioli too, should have their foliage cut back and the corms carefully dried for storing in paper bags.

Continue lifting and dividing hardy herbaceous perennials this month unless you live in a very cold area in which case it's better left until the spring.

✺ **'BUDGET TIP'** Always try to make use of new plant material that nature is offering to you free of charge. Prise any baby corms or cormlets off gladioli, for example, and store them separately for you will be able to raise new plants from these if you plant them in pots in the spring.

VEGETABLES

In most years, outdoor tomatoes are best cleared away at the beginning of September. But never waste green tomatoes – and never imagine that they can be used only for chutney. Even fairly immature specimens will ripen, given some warmth. Carefully harvest them all therefore, store them somewhere cool (but not for more than a few days in a fridge) and ripen them a few at a time either on a sunny window sill or in the airing cupboard.

Around the end of September, the bulk of your maincrop potatoes (and any earlies still left in the ground) can be dug for storing. Leave them briefly to dry off and then place them in paper bags or cardboard boxes. They must not be stored in plastic bags, which cause them to sweat and rot. Store them somewhere frost free – inside the north wall of a shed or garage is ideal because the temperature fluctuation there will be relatively slight.

Once large crops such as potatoes and tomatoes are cleared it is sensible to do autumn digging on areas not used as deep beds (see p. 59) and to fork on plenty of manure or compost. Never try to break down large clods at this stage. Nature will do it for you free and a fine soil surface will soon become compacted during the winter. If you are using deep beds, these too will benefit from having manure or compost forked onto the surface. Worms will take it down into the soil for you without charge.

❀ **'BUDGET TIP'** Encourage your crops to produce higher yields by putting cloches over your winter lettuce and endive and also, if you have enough, over the winter hardy spring onions and parsley too.

FRUIT

If you are picking fruit for storage, select them carefully. It's pointless storing damaged specimens as they will simply spread decay to others nearby. Apples and pears should be stored separately because pears need to be checked regularly whereas apples don't. For the same reason, pears are best stored individually in old wooden trays while apples are better in tens or dozens, in clean, plastic bags containing a few holes.

❀ **'BUDGET TIP'** Save money by reusing clean, plastic, fruit and vegetable bags containing a few holes to allow your stored apples to breathe and so remain in good condition.

If you belong to a gardening society, you might consider persuading them to invest in a fruit crusher. A very good crusher and press could be bought by an average sized society if all members contributed a couple of pounds. And believe me, it would be used for 24 hours a day at this time of year.

❀ **'BUDGET TIP'** A wise and thrifty tip is to convert windfall apples into delicious apple juice which can then be frozen and kept for months.

SEPTEMBER

The strawberry plants potted up from runners that you pegged down in July (see p. 76) can now be planted into their final positions, be these in containers or in the open ground.

TREES AND SHRUBS

Leaves will be beginning to drop from trees before the month is out. Rake them up regularly before they block drains and gutters. Remember to use them to make leaf mould (see p. 90), the finest mulching material of all.

❀ **'BUDGET TIP'** Save money by making your own mulch from leaves. Never waste them by putting them in the dustbin and never make bonfires with them; it is a most antisocial activity.

Check trees for any broken and jagged branch stubs which will provide places where decay fungi can enter and cause costly damage. Use a fine saw to make neat, straight cuts, just above the basal collar at the base of the branch. But don't try to seal the wound; let the tree do it naturally.

❀ **'BUDGET TIP'** If you buy trees or shrubs in containers on impulse because they are good value but won't be able to have a prepared place for them for some time, plant them temporarily, still in their containers – so that your investment is safeguarded and they are protected from penetrating frost.

Check the stakes on young trees to be sure they are secure before the full strength of the autumn winds strikes.

CLIMBERS

Self-clinging climbers such as ivies are splendid but can threaten to take over both your windows and your roof. Don't try to trim them with pruners, however, because you will blunt the blades. Use an old knife and run this along the brickwork about 20 cm (8 in) away from the edge of the wall and then pull off the severed shoots.

THE PAINTBOX OF AUTUMN

PLANT OF THE MONTH FOR OCTOBER

Parthenocissus tricuspidata 'Veitchii' (Boston ivy)

WHEN WE THINK of autumn colours, we tend to think of trees and shrubs but in practice the richest autumn colours in my garden belong to this self-clinging climber. The pale green leaves turn the most fiery of reds before dropping, almost all at the same time. It is vigorous, ultimately quite capable of reaching 7 m (23 ft), but can easily be trimmed back to keep it within bounds. Nothing else so attractively covers a bare and uninteresting wall. There are no leaves of course in the winter but the stems which are self-clinging and so do not need tying to a wall, do offer a pleasing pattern on the brickwork. To my mind, the alternative approach to concealing an uninteresting wall – using evergreen climbers such as ivy – whilst functional, offers nothing like as much variety through the months. 'Boston Ivy' is very self sufficient, growing in almost any type of soil and like most of the best climbers, it tolerates considerable dryness.

J	F	M	A	M	J	J	A	S	O	N	D
			L	L	L	L	L	L	L		

F flowers, L leaves, Fr fruit, S stems [ ] denotes in some years

TREES FOR THE BUDGET GARDEN

Most gardeners are only ever likely to buy one or two trees and so it is particularly important that they make the best choice – an incorrect decision can be very costly to put right later. On the other hand, once the correct choice *is* made, no other single type of plant can possibly provide you with such a good return for your money and make such an impact on your garden. And I always feel that October is the month when trees

OCTOBER

are most appreciated for it is now that those with autumn leaf colours are at their very finest.

CHOOSING A TREE There is no hard and fast distinction between a tree and a shrub but a good rule of thumb is that a tree exceeds about 6 m (20 ft) in height and is on a single stem. Many of the criteria used when choosing shrubs (see p. 91) are also relevant when you select a tree but, because you will probably have only one or two trees in your garden, the possible candidates must be assessed that much more rigorously.

Before you consider any other factor a tree's ultimate size must be taken into account. It is so easy to be seduced by a beautiful specimen in your garden centre and overlook the fact that it increases in height at 60 cm (2 ft) a year and will ultimately darken the neighbourhood. The table opposite gives my top dozen trees for small, budget gardens with their growth rates and ultimate heights but, if you are considering a tree not on my list, I do urge you first to check its growth rate in at least two good tree books – it is surprising how even experts can differ in this area and I find nursery labels can underestimate heights quite remarkably. Don't imagine that you can keep a vigorous tree within bounds by pruning; choose one that will stay small and not cast deep shade.

GOOD-VALUE FEATURES Let's then look a little more closely at some of the cost-effective and time-saving features that a tree can offer. Blossom is appealing but for most types of tree it lasts only a brief period and unfortunately some of the trees that are prettiest in flower – ornamental cherries most notably – are poor value because they are surprisingly dull for the rest of the year.

Flowering period is important too: many trees flower in the late spring when there is a good deal of other colour to be seen. If your garden is predominantly a spring garden therefore, with masses of bulbs, it will be well worth choosing a tree that flowers at some other period.

Many types of tree have attractive fruits, almost invariably later in the season when other garden colours are fading. So a tree that you see in a friend's garden in summer with relatively insignificant blossom might be saving its real glory until later. And remember too that most berries and other fruits are red, so a tree with orange, yellow, pink or white berries will always be eye-catching.

Foliage is very important in the budget garden too, in more ways than might seem obvious. An evergreen tree would appear to offer you most all-year-round appeal, but small evergreen trees with foliage that is other than pretty dull are few and far between. Most small evergreen trees that also have attractive blossom are generally on the tender side. Many conifers have rather pretty foliage but no blossom at all. Among

OCTOBER

deciduous trees a small, interestingly shaped leaf is important – not just because it is more pleasing to the eye but because large leaves cascading into a small garden can cause all manner of problems by blocking drains and making pathways slippery. But good autumn leaf colour is also extremely important, and this is best assessed by looking now at trees in

Trees for small, budget gardens

[handwritten: Purple. Bloodsgood   Green   OSAKAZUKI £25·]

TREE	HEIGHT After 10 years	Ultimate	FEATURES
Acer japonicum (Japanese maple)	2 m (6 ft 6 in)	3 m (10 ft)	Autumn colour, flowers insignificant
Amelanchier lamarckii (Shadberry) *[✓]*	6 m (20 ft)	10 m (33 ft)	Spring blossom, autumn colour, delicate form
Caragana arborescens 'Walker' (Weeping pea tree) *[✗]*	4 m (13 ft)	8 m (26 ft)	Yellow, pea-like, spring flowers, weeping habit
Cornus controversa 'Variegata' (Wedding cake tree) *[handwritten: large shrub]*	3 m (10 ft)	8 m (26 ft)	Variegated foliage, white summer blossom, tiered form
Crataegus laevigata 'Paul's Scarlet' (Hawthorn, May) *[✓]*	6 m (20 ft)	8 m (26 ft)	Double, pink flowers spring/early summer
Ilex aquifolium 'Bacciflava'† (Holly)	4 m (13 ft)	6 m (20 ft)	Yellow berries
Magnolia stellata (Star magnolia)	2 m (6 ft 6 in)	4 m (13 ft)	White, star-flowers in spring

[handwritten: Water lilly]

Malus 'Golden Hornet' (Crab apple) *[✓]*	*	*	Small, golden crab apples
Pyrus salicifolia 'Pendula' (Pear)	5 m (17 ft)	8 m (26 ft)	Silvery foliage, weeping habit
Robinia pseudoacacia 'Frisia' (False acacia, Locust) *[✗]*	6 m (20 ft)	12 m (40 ft)	Yellow foliage, flowers insignificant
Salix matsudana 'Tortuosa' (Corkscrew willow) *[✗]*	6 m (20 ft)	10 m (33 ft)	Intriguing twisted stems
Sorbus 'Joseph Rock' *[✓]*	5 m (17 ft)	10 m (33 ft)	Yellow berries

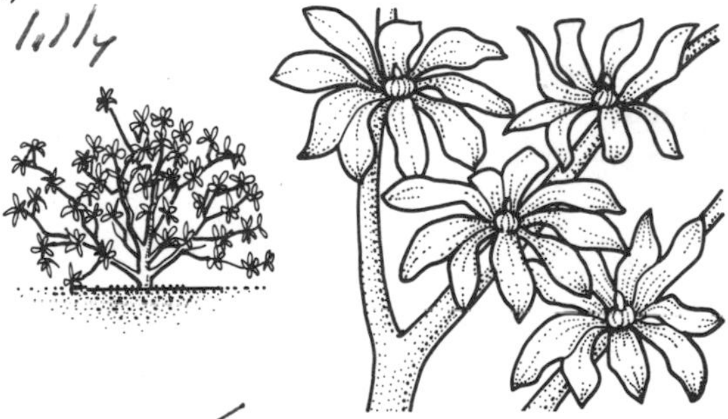

* size depends on the type of apple rootstock on to which the tree is grafted (see p. 110)
† evergreen

[handwritten: (Cashmeriana)   Vilmorinii   Sorbus, 99   Sorbus   WINTER CHEER.]

OCTOBER

your friends' gardens, the garden centre or in your local park.

<u>PLANTING A TREE</u> October is the month when tree planting is most satisfactorily done. Once you have chosen your tree, plant it with care. It will then not only establish quickly but also give you years of pleasure in return for your investment. The planting site must first be considered.

Whilst most trees will do no harm to the foundations of your house it is wise to be careful especially on heavy clay soils subject to shrinkage in dry weather. Because I am very cautious, I never plant a tree closer to a house than a distance roughly equal to its ultimate height. If you already have an established tree closer than this, please don't worry, although, if it is a large weeping willow or a large species of poplar, it might be worth asking for an opinion from your local authority as the roots of these trees are notorious at invading drains.

Prepare the planting position very carefully. Dig a hole at least twice the size of the container in which the tree has grown and work in plenty of compost or other organic matter and a handful of general fertilizer. Insert a wooden stake on the windward side so that the tree is blown away from the stake, not onto it. Ease the root ball from the container, gently tease out the roots at the edge to encourage them to grow outwards and then firm the soil around it.

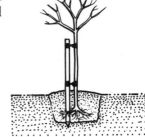

❀ **'BUDGET TIP'** A good rustic pole will prove as effective a tree stake as any costly length of squared timber – but do treat the lower part of the pole thoroughly with preservative.

Tie the trunk carefully to the stake using a proper belt-style tie which will not chafe. After spending good money on your tree, I do feel it will be worth a few more pence. If you can't find or afford one however, an old pair of tights will do the job fairly well. Whatever you do, don't use string or wire which will cut in to the bark. Thereafter water the tree very well and continue to give water every week for a month or so, especially if the weather is dry. Do keep the area around the tree free from weeds so that soil nutrients are absorbed only by the tree.

LABOUR-SAVING HINTS FOR THE GARDEN

Not many amateurs would willingly garden full time. Even for those who consider it their number one hobby, there is a limit to the hours that they want to spend weeding, watering, feeding, mowing and trimming, enjoyable as planting, seed sowing and harvesting crops might be. I'm sure that we all have an interest in using our time most efficiently – and time well spent very often means money saved too. And people who are elderly, infirm or handicapped naturally have a special reason for wanting their gardening to be as labour-saving and easy as possible.

At this time of the year, with so many tasks waiting for our attention before the winter, efficient gardening becomes a priority. I have always believed that the best way to make your garden labour-efficient is to consider those aspects that occupy most time – and then eliminate them.

FILLING LARGE AREAS ECONOMICALLY The larger a garden the more it is likely to be time-consuming to manage. But the cheapest and simplest way to manage a large area is by grassing it – although not with a neatly trimmed lawn. Confine close mowing to a small area near the house and treat the remainder as rough grass. This requires much less frequent mowing and can be used as the basis of an attractive planting with native flowers, which themselves benefit from being left unmown until late in the summer (see p. 72). Bulbs, especially daffodils and narcissi, allowed to naturalize in the grass, will provide delightful spring colour with almost no requirement for routine maintenance. In fact, any types of bulb that do not require annual lifting are well worthwhile.

In large gardens I certainly wouldn't suggest blanket 'hard gardening' – covering the entire area with paving, gravel or a similar non-plant surface – but, as countless thousands of pretty little inner city gardens bear witness, it can be valuable in gardens where a lawn would soon be reduced to a quagmire in winter. And plants may be grown in large containers on such a surface to provide a most attractive appearance.

REDUCING MAINTENANCE ON PERENNIALS Ornamental trees and shrubs for the most part need little attention, even in containers; the majority will thrive perfectly well with little or no pruning and are good value for money. Climbing plants are slightly more labour-intensive for there are very few that will provide good colour and cover without at least some pruning. Nonetheless, in less formal positions, where they may be allowed freer rein, some types of clematis for instance will be effective (see p. 28).

REDUCING MAINTENANCE ON ANNUALS All plants grown as annuals are labour intensive in some way. The work involved in raising them yourself from seed can of course be avoided by buying trays of young plants from a garden centre but this can be very expensive. You will also still be faced with the chore of hardening them off, planting them out and watering and liquid feeding them regularly throughout the summer. Set against these drawbacks is the undeniable appeal of the almost instant colour that bedding plants provide. Thus, if time and money are in short supply, use

OCTOBER

them in small areas close to the house; and if watering will present problems, limit your choice to the slightly more robust types such as pelargoniums, fibrous rooted begonias and busy lizzies.

After watering and feeding, the gardening operation most consuming of time is weeding but if you adopt more permanent plantings of herbaceous perennials or trees and shrubs, weed control can be all but eliminated. I have proved it myself. The answer lies quite simply in mulching, the finest weed suppressing technique of all (see p. 88).

Much of what I have said about bedding plants applies to vegetables too. They will not thrive without constant watering and you will also have the additional work involved in weeding between the rows and in the beds. Among the least labour intensive vegetable crops are the roots such as carrots and parsnips but they are also among the most difficult to grow, requiring very careful soil preparation. It is perfectly possible to grow satisfactory crops of French beans, radishes, lettuces and other small leafy crops such as spinach with only once a week attention to watering in a dry summer. But peas, runner beans and most of the larger crop plants such as potatoes, cauliflowers, broccoli and Brussels sprouts all require additional attention in the form of feeding, staking or some other special cultural technique and are best avoided by anyone with limited time.

Paving is probably the best surface for a small garden where a lawn might be difficult to maintain properly, and the addition of containers in a variety of shapes and sizes and interesting plants can be most attractive.

OCTOBER

GARDENS FOR THOSE WITH A DISABILITY The special problems related to gardening with some form of handicap have fortunately become much more widely recognized in recent years and several organizations exist to cater especially for such needs. There are two aspects to the subject: the design of the garden itself and the tools and techniques to be used. Let's just look at some of the commonest problems:

● Wheelchairs will not readily go up and down steps nor through narrow gates;

● A person confined to a wheelchair cannot readily reach – they require long-handled tools or the garden itself must be brought up to their level by means of raised beds (see p. 39).

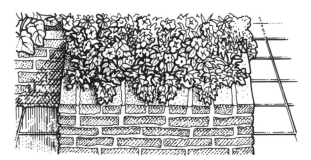

A wide range of flowers and plants can be grown in a raised bed.

● Long-handled tools can be heavy and difficult to manipulate – many wheelchair gardeners have not only impaired mobility but impaired strength too – so they must be lightweight and should if possible incorporate some lever or other principle by which work can be achieved for less effort.

Blind or partially sighted gardeners will derive delight from selections of plants that are perfumed but there are other considerations too. The sense of touch is also important and plants that are pleasing to handle – perhaps through their possession of silky foliage – will be appreciated; especially if this handling is associated with the release of a perfume. Conversely it is important to avoid sticky, prickly or otherwise unpleasant types of vegetation in a garden for those with visual defects.

BULBS

Bulbs are wonderful value for they are probably the only garden plants that I would guarantee to provide a superb display of flowers so soon after you have bought them. The problems generally come in the second and subsequent years when the display begins to decline and they are no longer proving such good value for money. I shall discuss ways to prevent this under 'Planting bulbs', but first, a word about choosing them.

OCTOBER

CHOOSING BULBS Although you will see advertisements for mail order bulb offers at this time of year, I always advise personal shopping if possible. You will save on the cost of postage but, more importantly, you can buy from a serve-yourself stand and actually see the quality of your purchases which may save money in the long run. Try to visit your garden centre as soon as the new season's supplies come in and you will then be able to choose the largest, plumpest bulbs. You will pay a fixed amount for a standard-sized brown paper bag which you can then fill yourself.

❀ **'BUDGET TIP'** With daffodils especially, select those with two tips – or 'noses' as they are called – as these will produce more flowers.

❀ **'BUDGET TIP'** If cost saving is very important take a chance and wait until early November when daffodils, narcissi and crocuses will generally be reduced in price but will still flower in the following spring if they are planted promptly (tulips are less likely to be reduced in price until the New Year by which time it is really becoming a little late to plant other types of bulb).

❀ **'BUDGET TIP'** Mixed varieties of daffodils in particular will always be cheaper than pure strains but conversely will never give as good a display because the blooms of the later-flowering types will be pushing up among the unsightly dead heads of the earlier ones.

When choosing bulbs, try to select those varieties that are indicated on the labels as 'good for naturalizing' as these will multiply in your garden.

PLANTING BULBS Bulbs will grow well in most types of soil other than those that are constantly wet, but it is a good idea to place a little sand under the bulbs when you plant them in order to lessen the likelihood of rotting. Use a trowel for planting and as a general rule, place the bulbs with their base at a depth equal to roughly three times their diameter.

Growing bulbs in grass around the bases of trees and shrubs is very attractive but should be done carefully. Lift a patch of turf before planting and replace it afterwards. Don't make the mistake of planting bulbs in

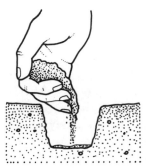
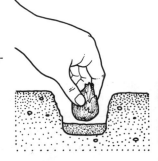

Left: place some sand in the base of the hole to stop the bulbs rotting. *Right:* sit the bulb comfortably on the sand.

OCTOBER

lawns where the grass will be regularly mown. In general, bulb foliage should not be cut down until about six weeks after the flowers have faded and during this time, the plants should be given several doses of liquid fertilizer. Failing to do either of these tasks, together with planting too shallowly or in dense shade are the commonest reasons why so many bulbs fade away after the first year.

Although planting bulbs to naturalize is much the best way of using them, there are a few exceptions. The large-flowered tulips are poor value because they must be lifted each year, dried off carefully and replanted again in the autumn. Even then, they are usually poor shadows of their original selves.

❀ **'BUDGET TIP'** If you enjoy tulips, my advice is to grow the species such as *Tulipa tarda* which will naturalize and grow on from year to year.

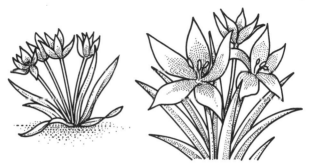

Bulbs of most types can be grown in containers but inevitably they must be lifted to make way for summer bedding plants. They can be replanted in autumn but, because of this disturbance to their roots, they will need especial attention giving to their feeding. Bulbs planted in containers can also be artificially induced to flower early (see p. 84).

PROPAGATING BULBS A clump of bulbs can be divided in a similar manner to herbaceous perennials and so will prove very cost-effective. Carefully pull apart bulbs and replant them individually. Although it is possible to cut up daffodil and other bulbs, this is a chancy business and you may well lose the lot. Lilies are exceptions however. Their bulbs are expensive and even though they can be grown from seed, it will take five years or so before they reach flowering size.

❀ **'BUDGET TIP'** An economical way to multiply your lily stock is to buy one bulb of your chosen lily and pull away from it about half a dozen fleshy scales around the bulb. Pop them in a small plastic bag of soil-less compost and hang them up in the airing cupboard with a clothes peg. Keep an eye open for the appearance of any green shoots; then as these appear plant the scales up in small pots of compost and set on the window-ledge. Water moderately and give liquid feed whilst the plants are in leaf. They should reach flowering size in a couple of years.

OCTOBER

JOBS FOR OCTOBER

GENERAL

Tetanus is a very serious but easily preventable disease, often present in soil and very common in some parts of the British Isles. Unless there is some sound medical reason to the contrary, everyone who gardens or handles soil should have regular injections against tetanus. It will cost you nothing but save you a great deal in terms of peace of mind and prevention of possible illness. See your GP who will advise you.

THE INDOOR GARDEN

At the end of October take a look at the hyacinths that you buried outdoors to check if the green shoots are beginning to elongate. If they are, then continue as I outlined on p. 84; if not, then re-bury them for a further week or two.

CONTAINERS

Spring flowering bulbs may now be planted in containers (see p. 104). When you are planting containers with more than one type of bulb do give some thought to flowering times and colour matching.

If you have set up winter hanging baskets, remember that they will not need as much water as summer baskets and can indeed easily become waterlogged in cold weather.

If you have any terracotta pots that are doubtfully frost-proof, don't take a chance. They cost a great deal of money and are best put safely away in the shed or garage where deterioration will be minimal.

❁ **'BUDGET TIP'** To prevent terracotta pots from jamming together and cracking, put layers of newspaper between them when they are stacked.

GREENHOUSES, COLD FRAMES AND CLOCHES

If you are growing winter lettuce plants under cloches, it is wise to try to deter slugs from reaching them first. A barrier of ash or soot around the plants will help to dissuade them – and of course will be protected from the rain under the cover of the cloche itself.

If you have a heater of any sort in your greenhouse, do check that it is working efficiently before the cold weather really arrives. Paraffin heaters should have the wicks carefully trimmed – and renewed if necessary.

When putting plants in greenhouses or cold frames for winter protection, don't crowd them too close together as this will simply bring about stagnant air and encourage mould growth.

On mild days from now on, it is important that the greenhouse, cold frame and, if possible, cloches too, are opened and given some ventilation. But do close them up again at night.

LAWN

Lawn mowing can continue provided the weather is mild and the ground not too wet, but do have the mower blades set at their highest.

Lawns can be raked lightly to pull out any thatch of dead grass and moss. You will be amazed at how much material is removed even by a light raking, but it can all be put to use in the compost bin. Don't be tempted to rake too vigorously, however, or you will pull out pieces of turf.

THE FLOWER GARDEN

Herbaceous perennials should be cut down this month in order to tidy up the borders for winter but if there are any with seeding heads, do leave them for the birds to feed on. I suggest this not just out of the kindness of my heart, but because it may also serve the purpose of diverting their attention from the buds on your fruit bushes.

As you clear the borders, do take care of canes or other plant supports. They must be cleaned, *dried* and then kept somewhere dry for re-use again next year. Don't make the mistake of leaving twig supports out in the open as they will attract coral spot disease which can then spread to your trees and shrubs; storing them in the dry is essential.

❀ **'BUDGET TIP'** It would be a great shame to lose your valuable rock garden plants so carefully trim off any damaged leaves. These will attract moisture and decay in the coming weeks.

If you were able to grow any wallflowers and sweet williams (see p. 64), or even if you have to buy some, now is the time to put them in their permanent flowering positions ready for next spring.

Spring flowering bulbs are now in the shops and should be planted as soon as possible (see p. 104), although it is wise to wait until November before planting tulips. They can start into premature growth if planted early and are then prone to frost damage.

VEGETABLES

Clear away any remains of summer vegetable crops promptly. Moribund plants left in the ground over winter will serve no purpose except for harbouring pests and diseases, which will involve extra expense and simply add to your problems next year.

OCTOBER

When you cut down old runner bean plants, leave the roots in the ground as they have tiny nitrogen producing nodules which will slowly decay and release nutrient into the soil. You can do the same with other members of the pea and bean family.

Unless you have had root disease problems on your runner beans the next crop can go in the same place. The trench for them is best dug in October before hard frosts make it difficult, with plenty of compost and other organic matter forked in as you do so.

FRUIT

Trim raspberry canes before the worst of the weather arrives. Cut off the tips to leave them approximately 2 m (6 ft 6 in) tall, or to the top of the support post or wires.

Continue to pick apples for storing and eating and do try to store them somewhere away from strong smells such as paint and petrol.

✿ **'BUDGET TIP'** If you are planning to buy fruit trees visit some local pick-your-own farms in October where you will discover the ones which grow well in your area and sample the best-flavoured varieties (see p. 109).

TREES AND SHRUBS

Continue raking up fallen leaves regularly (see p. 88). If you have vast quantities of them and there are too many even for your leaf mould cage, fork them into the surface of herbaceous and shrub borders where they will gradually be pulled down by earthworms over the winter. This will help to improve your soil structure and give you better crops next year.

Rose bushes may well have long, whippy shoots that could be blown around in the winter wind and rock the plant in the ground. Therefore cut these shoots back now to prevent damage to the plants – but don't do the main pruning until the spring.

Complete all hedge clipping by the middle of October. If you cut after then, you stand a chance of exposing soft tissues to severe frosts with the result that the hedge could appear unsightly and die back in places.

Visit public parks or gardens with good tree collections to see the autumn colours and perhaps find ideas that would suit your garden.

CLIMBERS

Although the best time to prune clematis is in the spring, it might be worthwhile cutting back some growth now on very vigorous later-flowering types such as *Clematis tangutica* as they can be battered by winter gales.

COOL AND MISTY

PLANT OF THE MONTH FOR NOVEMBER

Polypodium vulgare **'Cornubiense'**

Hardy ferns are a good choice for the budget gardener who can't devote much time to the garden. Over the years ferns have waxed and waned in gardeners' affections but they are now very much on the ascendent again. They do not of course have flowers although many species do bear attractive patterning beneath the leaves caused by the spore-bearing bodies. Best of all the hardy ferns are the evergreen species and varieties and, among them, *Polypodium vulgare* 'Cornubiense' is one of the finest. It is not too big (reaching about 30 × 30 cm/12 × 12 in in three years) and has the most fresh looking light green leaves. Moreover, unlike the majority of ferns, it doesn't need damp, acidic conditions. In a good, rich soil it will luxuriate and provide interest at the front of a border or in a special corner all year through.

J	F	M	A	M	J	J	A	S	O	N	D
L	L	L	L	L	L	L	L	L	L	L	L

F flowers, L leaves, Fr fruit, S stems [ ] denotes in some years

PLANNING A FRUIT GARDEN

Above all else in the garden, November means planting fruit trees and bushes. For, if fresh vegetables are expensive, fresh fruit are even more so, especially out of season. Yet they are among the easiest of all edible crops to grow, requiring the very minimum of attention. And they can also be kept for long periods – several varieties of apple will store for months while almost all types of fruit can be frozen simply and effectively. Moreover, unlike many vegetables, fruit plants can make a significant contribution to the aesthetic appearance of your garden – to my mind, no ornamental tree matches an apple in full blossom. And given dwarf

NOVEMBER

varieties and containers it is perfectly possible to grow fruit plants on path edges and on paved areas even if you have no garden at all.

Unfortunately it isn't possible to raise fruit plants from seed and even producing them from cuttings is a very chancy business, which is unlikely to result in anything worthwhile. As they are to be important features of your garden for many years, it really is worth investing in the best quality you can afford.

Pear tree blossom.

CHOOSING AN APPLE ROOTSTOCK VARIETY There are three main garden fruit trees: apples, plums and pears. This order also roughly reflects the simplicity of growing them. Apples are the easiest, because they are the hardiest and one variety or other will thrive in almost any part of the British Isles. Also important for small, budget gardens is the fact that apple varieties are available grafted on to dwarfing rootstocks, probably the most cost-saving development in the history of fruit-tree growing. As this important fact still causes gardeners some confusion, it's worth a little explanation.

When you buy a fruit tree, whatever the variety, it will not be growing on its own roots. It will have been grafted on to the roots of a quite different variety, called a rootstock variety, that has been bred not for its fruit production but for its ability to form good anchorage. Now, by one of the miracles of nature, the rootstock variety dictates the ultimate size of the tree, regardless of the fruit variety and regardless of the way it is pruned.

Apple rootstock varieties of most interest to budget gardeners

ROOTSTOCK NUMBER	TREE HEIGHT AFTER 10 YEARS	MINIMUM SPACING BETWEEN PLANTS Free-standing	Cordon	FEATURES
M.27	1.5 m (5 ft)	1.5 m (5 ft)	0.75 m (2½ ft)	Needs very good soil and permanent stake
M.9	2.0 m (6 ft 6 in)	3.0 m (10 ft)	0.75 (2½ ft)	For general garden use; needs permanent stake
M.26	2.5 m (8 ft)	3.5 m (12 ft)	1.0 m (3 ft)	Tolerates poor soil

Rootstock varieties have numbers, not names. (The table lists apple rootstock varieties of most interest to gardeners, with the approximate sizes of the trees they will produce and the spacing to be used between free-standing trees and cordons.) Depending on the size of tree you want therefore and the space you have available, you should ask your nursery or garden centre for your chosen fruiting variety grafted on to the relevant rootstock. And don't forget that with limited room, apples on the rootstock M.27 can be grown most successfully in a half-barrel container (see p. 112).

Training fruit trees in cordon fashion enables you to grow several varieties within a very small area.

Even if you have no real garden at all, a small fruit tree on a modern dwarfing rootstock can be grown most effectively in a half barrel.

✣ **'BUDGET TIP'** The cordon is a particularly useful way of growing trees in limited space for it comprises a single stem trained against a wall or fence with horizontal support wires.

CHOOSING AN APPLE-FRUITING VARIETY The choice of a fruiting variety is of course very much a matter of personal taste but, unless you live in an inner city, it is very sensible first to visit the nearest pick-your-own fruit farm (see p. 108). The apples you are used to buying in the greengrocer or supermarket may well be different from those that grow locally. Do remember that with apples, two compatible varieties are required in order for pollination to occur which can be a drawback. To save the cost of buying two trees however, a good plan is to arrange for your neighbour to have one and for you to have the other – pollinating bees will be very happy to fly over the boundary fence.

✣ **'BUDGET TIP'** A wise and thrifty way to grow apples is to buy a family tree in which two (or sometimes more) varieties are grafted onto the same rootstock; the cost will be a little higher than having one tree but still less than

NOVEMBER

NOVEMBER

two separate ones. And a family tree has another money-saving bonus in that you can have both a dessert and a cooking variety on the same plant.

If you do strike up a pact with your neighbour or, if there are already suitable pollinating trees close by, and you can only have or need a single tree, choose a dual purpose apple such as 'Blenheim Orange', good both for eating and cooking.

PEARS AND PLUMS Unfortunately, pears and plums are not available on so-called dwarfing rootstocks – the best you can hope for are 'Quince C' for pears and 'Pixy' for plums. For this reason, they really aren't amenable to being grown in tubs but with limited space, they can be grown against a wall – cordon-trained for a pear and fan-trained for a plum.

❀ **'BUDGET TIP'** An important cost-effective bonus with plums is that the best (and I strongly recommend 'Victoria') are self-fertile so you need only one tree, while the pear 'Conference' is sufficiently self-fertile for you to obtain a good crop even if it has no mate.

SOFT FRUITS Soft fruits are even easier to grow than tree fruits and the cost benefits are greater still – even at the height of the season a punnet of raspberries isn't cheap. Whilst most good gardening books will tell you how to grow them in the open where they can take up precious garden room, I shall concentrate on an inexpensive way of producing good crops from limited space – by growing them in containers.

As with fruit trees, your fruit bushes will give best value for money if you use a decent-sized container and much the best and cheapest is my favourite wooden half-barrel. This should be positioned in full sun, in its intended resting place before being filled – moving one with half a ton of compost inside is not for the faint-hearted. I line the inside of the barrel with heavy duty plastic sheet, ensuring of course that there are several drainage holes – through both wood and sheet. A good compost is essential and two or three bags of John Innes No. 3, at least for the top half (see p. 50) will be money well spent.

❀ **'BUDGET TIP'** Save money on container liners by cutting up old, heavy-weight plastic bags.

STRAWBERRIES Strawberries are particularly successful in containers and mine do extremely well in a wooden half-barrel.

❀ **'BUDGET TIP'** Avoid extravagant expenditure on costly and fiddling strawberry tubs with holes in the side. These purpose made tubs are also much more expensive to fill as you really do need proper compost from top to bottom.

To obtain even better value from your strawberry plants grow varieties that will crop in succession from very early to very late – and not just around Wimbledon fortnight. My suggested strawberries for high yield with good flavour and several years cropping are:
- 'Cambridge Favourite'
- 'Silver Jubilee'
- 'Tenira' and
- 'Aromel'

BUSH AND CANE FRUIT Perhaps the area of fruit production that has been adapted least to container culture is among the bush and cane fruits but they will all crop very well. Red, white and blackcurrants and gooseberries give fine crops, either in half-barrels or even in slightly smaller containers. The compact blackcurrant variety 'Ben Sarek' is excellent and my preferences for the others are:
- 'Stanza' (red currant)
- 'White Versailles' (white currant) and
- 'Invicta' (gooseberry – a variety that fulfils another of my cost-saving criteria in being resistant to mildew and therefore not needing to be sprayed).

Raspberries might seem impossible for containers but even they can be grown in threes in tubs and trained to a stout, central post. Pruning and pest control are naturally carried out in exactly the same manner as if the plants are growing in a garden bed. Choose the variety 'Glen Clova' for good yields, good flavour and ease of cultivation.

❧ **'BUDGET TIP'** Profitability and success are easy to come by if you use a little inventiveness and ingenuity and remember the golden rules of growing any plant in such a confined manner. You *must* pay extra attention to feeding and to watering – a good mulch on the surface of the compost is extremely cost-effective.

GARDEN BOUNDARIES

Unless you live on a completely open-plan housing estate you need some form of boundary to your garden. A boundary:
- Gives privacy;
- Protects you and your garden from the wind;
- Keeps out the neighbour's livestock; and
- Keeps in your own dog and, possibly, cat (although keeping cats where they belong is more a matter for a magician than a gardener).

And, as winter and winter winds threaten, this is an excellent time to think about your garden boundaries and if they are adequate for the purpose intended.

NOVEMBER

The ideal boundary should comprise at least 50 per cent holes so that it will break the force of the wind whilst still providing protection and resilience.

Planning is a very important factor because the garden boundary that fulfils most of the necessary criteria can very easily prove to be the most expensive. Let's assume therefore that you are starting from scratch with the bare minimum that many builders erect in the form of a concrete post-and-wire boundary marker. The most economical way to make it dog and small child proof is by attaching chicken wire to the posts.

❀ **'BUDGET TIP'** The cheapest chicken wire is that with the largest mesh – wire netting with 50 mm (2 in) holes is less than half the price of that with holes of 13 mm ($^1/_2$ in). And not surprisingly the longer the roll, the relatively cheaper it becomes – yet another reason for clubbing together with neighbours to buy in bulk.

Once in position, chicken wire can be disguised very prettily and cheaply with climbers, such as clematis, but do avoid the very vigorous varieties such as *Clematis montana* and certainly steer clear of the Russian vine (*Polygonum baldschuanicum*), which will very quickly swamp not only the fence, but also half the garden.

❀ **'BUDGET TIP'** A cost-effective cat deterrent for a fenced or walled garden it to stretch a single strand of wire about 6 cm ($2^1/_4$ in) above the top of the fence. Cats will then find it very difficult to balance.

FENCE PANELS After wire netting, fence panels are the next cheapest type of boundary – but cheapness here is a relative term and new panels are still pretty costly. Second-hand ones are pretty useless unfortunately as they will almost inevitably have been weakened in the course of dismantling and re-erection. Any fence moreover suffers a major financial drawback in being all but impermeable to the wind and therefore prone to damage.

If you already have a fence however, especially one of overlapping softwood panels, make the most of it by giving it adequate support.

❀ **'BUDGET TIPS'** Save money by using second-hand wood for your fence posts. Almost any small ads listing in a local paper will direct you to someone who supplies old timber, and a call to a local builder or demolition contractor will also prove fruitful.

You need stout wooden posts to act as diagonal braces for every second vertical post of your fence. Thoroughly soak the bottom of the braces in creosote, ram them against the fence and secure them with long screws.

NOVEMBER

A boring fence, or even a rather low one that offers little privacy, can be improved by fixing wooden trellis panels to the top and then training climbers up the vertical posts and along the trellis. Do be sure to fix the trellis securely, however, as it will be exposed to the force of the wind.

HEDGES In so many ways however, the most cost-effective and successful boundary is a hedge which offers all of the criteria of privacy, toughness, wind permeability and yet also offers a haven for birds and other wildlife. The drawbacks, I can hear you saying, are the time taken for it to establish and the cost. I think I can help on both counts. To give some protection whilst your hedge is growing, plant it alongside your fence – you will generally find that by the time the hedge has reached the desired height, the fence will be coming to the end of its days. There is a temptation to speed up hedge establishment by planting Leyland cypress – the fastest moving thing that isn't actually classed as Formula 1.

Hedges should be planted carefully, with very good soil preparation. This way, they will establish and thicken quickly. It helps to secure the young plants to a wire.

❀ **'BUDGET TIP'** It is a false economy to use very fast-growing plants so that a hedge becomes quickly established. Such plants don't stop when you might wish them to but continue heading upwards to give you a continuing and increasingly difficult and time-consuming task of trimming.

Choose a conifer if you will – they are relatively cheap after all – but select a variety of Lawson cypress or even of thuja, a much under-rated and rather attractive scented cypress-like plant.

On the matter of cost, go to your garden centre or nursery and you will find that container-grown Lawson cypress or thuja around 60 cm (2 ft) tall will cost about £3 each. It doesn't take much arithmetic to work out that, with plants spaced 60 cm (2 ft) apart, even a short length of hedge will prove a costly undertaking. Yet bare-rooted plants of similar size cost around £15–20 per 100 from wholesale horticultural nurseries. Even with a delivery charge the savings will be vast and better still if, once again, you can place an order with a friend. The only drawback is that as the plants are bare-rooted they must be planted on arrival – although even then they could be planted temporarily in their bundles until your planting position is ready.

NOVEMBER

❀ **'BUDGET TIP'** A very thrifty and wise way to buy hedging plants is from a bulk supplier. Look in your Yellow Pages or the small ads of a reputable gardening journal for the address of your local wholesale horticultural nursery.

RENOVATING AN OLD HEDGE Severely overgrown conifer hedges can't be rejuvenated very well as they don't readily produce new shoots from old wood. You can cut them down to the required height but you will always have bare areas at the base. Growing an attractive climber such as a variegated ivy to cover the bare stems is the best answer. Other types of hedge such as beech, privet or hawthorn will regenerate well, however, and you can cut them back pretty hard. After such severe pruning, always give the hedge a generous application of general purpose fertilizer and if possible a good watering.

JOBS FOR NOVEMBER

GENERAL

If you have a glut of fresh produce at the end of the season, a freezable variety can save you money. Therefore, as you choose vegetable seed varieties from catalogues, look out especially for those described as suitable for freezing. With some types of vegetable, there is a considerable difference between varieties in the success with which they freeze.

THE INDOOR GARDEN

Watering can all but stop on cacti and succulents while other house plants should be given very little. Although your house may be warm in the daytime, the temperature will drop greatly at night and this is when waterlogged compost becomes very cold and damage to roots occurs.

Move plants away from window panes and bring them inside the curtains at night – the air between curtains and glass can become very cold indeed.

CONTAINERS

Keep a careful watch on your winter containers as watering them isn't easy to judge. If they contain small plants, with a fair amount of soil exposed, then they can easily become waterlogged. If on the other hand, the plants are large and the soil is covered with foliage, then even heavy winter rains may not penetrate and the soil can dry out.

GREENHOUSES, COLD FRAMES AND CLOCHES

Make a point of *not* going into the greenhouse on cold mornings. You will almost instantly cause the temperature inside to drop several degrees. An unheated greenhouse can build up warmth again only slowly when the weak winter sun comes out whilst a heater will use a great deal of extra fuel in trying to make up for the loss.

Continue to pull off any dead or yellowed leaves from plants being overwintered under any sort of protection. A weekly check on *mild* days should become a routine.

LAWN

As in October, lawn work can continue but only during mild and fairly dry weather. In any event, it's sensible not to use equipment on the lawn early in the morning as there will almost invariably be heavy dew and, as you work, your lovely green turf will turn to less than lovely, brown mud.

You will often see fairy rings of toadstools on the lawn at this time of year but they are no real cause for alarm. They can't be controlled and although they can cause some localized damage to the grass, this can generally be overcome by spiking with a fork in the worst affected areas. Don't be tempted to eat any of the toadstools as some very poisonous species can occur in the rings. And if you don't have expert guidance, don't eat *any* wild mushrooms. It may seem temptingly cost-saving but is not a risk for the inexperienced to take.

THE FLOWER GARDEN

Continue to cut back herbaceous perennials and tidy up borders. The few herbaceous perennials such as red-hot poker (*Kniphofia*) that are ever-green, however, will be damaged if they are cut back. Their leaves should carefully be tied up over the plant to give frost protection to the crown.

This is the best possible time to plant tulip bulbs. Follow the procedures outlined for planting other types of bulb (see p. 104) and do remember that they can be planted until well into next month.

❀ **'BUDGET TIP'** If you have primulas in the garden, pot up a few and bring them indoors. They will flower in time for Christmas. In due course, they can be returned to the garden.

Check your stored dahlia tubers for any signs of rotting. Cut off and destroy any damaged ones and then carefully re-pack the remainder.

VEGETABLES

If you have winter vegetables in the ground, either in the open or under cloches, do pull off any dead or yellowed leaves as soon as they become apparent. They will simply harbour diseases if left on the plants and may cost you your crop.

NOVEMBER

Continue with autumn digging as and when conditions allow. At this time of year, fresh manure may safely be put on to the soil. In spring, you must use rotted or composted material.

There is nothing to match the flavour of the first broad beans of the spring but they are always so expensive then. Save the money, by sowing some seeds now of the hardy, overwintering variety 'Aquadulce'. In many areas, broad beans will crop perfectly satisfactorily without protection but, in cold and wet parts of the British Isles, cover them with cloches.

FRUIT

As with trees and shrubs this is a good month to plant fruit of all types.

✿ **'BUDGET TIP'** Look out for special promotions at your local garden centre or shop. They can be a cheap way to replenish your garden stock.

Winter pruning of apple and pear trees can begin this month and can continue at any time through the winter, even if the weather is freezing – it makes for good exercise on cold days.

Continue to check your stored apples and remove any decayed ones.

TREES AND SHRUBS

In all except the coldest areas November is the best month for planting deciduous trees and shrubs of all kinds, including roses, as they should establish well before the really cold weather arrives. This is especially true of plants that are sold bare-rooted.

Continue taking hardwood cuttings (see p. 71) provided the temperature isn't actually freezing. Never help yourself to cuttings from plants in public parks or gardens although, if you ask, you may well be lucky and certainly if you happen to see one of the gardeners pruning or throwing out surplus material, they will always be pleased to let you have some.

If you find a hollow at the base of a tree or shrub stem caused by it having moved in the wind, re-secure the plant and fill the hollow with soil. Otherwise, water will collect there, freeze and so damage your plant.

CLIMBERS

Herbaceous climbers such as the lovely golden hop (*Humulus lupulus*) and Scots flame flower (*Tropaeolum speciosum*) should be cut back now to just above soil level. If you don't already grow these plants they are worth looking out for as they represent excellent value, give very rapid cover during summer and yet don't produce an ever-increasing massive, woody framework. They look splendid scrambling over conifer hedges.

FESTIVITIES

PLANT OF THE MONTH FOR DECEMBER

Helleborus foetidus (Stinking hellebore)

UNFORTUNATELY NAMED THE stinking hellebore (I am unsure why for I have never detected a smell from one), this is near the top of my list of versatile perennials. It is an evergreen with rich, dark green, glossy leaves and so is valuable on that count alone. But through the winter, when little else is in bloom, stinking hellebore has clusters of the most delightful, nodding, lime-green, bell-like flowers with purple tips. It must be the plant that has winter flowers for the longest period – well into spring. But it has other attributes too. It is very tough and the leaves will only be browned by the most intense frost and it thrives in conditions that most other plants shun – dry shade. I have it in various parts of my own garden, including a dry north-facing border. Stinking hellebore reaches about 60 cm (2 ft) in height and, apart from cutting back the old leaves as they gradually wither, it requires very little attention.

J	F	M	A	M	J	J	A	S	O	N	D
F	F	F	F							F	F
L	L	L	L	L	L	L	L	L	L	L	L

F flowers, L leaves, Fr fruit, S stems [ ] denotes in some years

CHOOSING AND CARING FOR GARDEN TOOLS

The somewhat more leisurely gardening period of the winter months affords time for new gardeners to plan ahead and assess how well-equipped they are for the coming season. But it is a good time, too, for the more experienced gardener to take stock of his or her tools, check that they have been cleaned and cared for and see which, if any, need replacing. There are of course gardeners who collect tools in the way that some people collect postage stamps but in practice, highly successful gardening, even in a fairly large garden, can be performed with a very short, basic list of equipment. A budget gardener should be able to manage with a fork, spade, trowel, hoe, rake and some cutting tools.

DECEMBER

It perhaps goes without saying that the cheapest tools are those that are bought second-hand. Beware, however, of buying tools that are seriously bent, missing tines or other parts or are in need of new handles. For the price of a replacement fork or spade handle, you can virtually obtain a set of modern inexpensive detachable head cultivators.

❀ **'BUDGET TIP'** The best sources for cheap gardening tools tend to be car boot sales or auctions, where bundles of old gardening tools can often be bought for a song.

FORKS AND SPADES The fork and spade should be of the small pattern generally called 'border' tools, but sometimes known as ladies' tools. These are cheaper and will be perfectly adequate for all except the largest vegetable plot. And, being smaller, are much easier and less tiring to manage too. Most modern gardeners find a D-shaped handle to be more comfortable than the older and traditional T-pattern. When buying a fork or spade:

● Check that the handle isn't loose;

● Check that the splice where it attaches to the business end is firm for this really isn't something that it's practical to tighten;

● Handle the tools before you buy them – no matter how good a bargain they appear to be. If they are too heavy for you, then you will never garden successfully and nor will you enjoy your gardening.

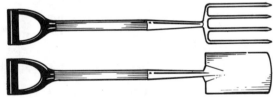

The 'D'-shaped handle is the most comfortable for many gardeners.

TROWELS A trowel is essential for planting all of your bedding plants, vegetables and in fact anything small enough to be held in your hand. The same criteria apply to choosing a trowel as to a fork or spade – do hold it first and do be sure that the handle doesn't spin round.

❀ **'BUDGET TIP'** Don't spend money on a hand (or weeding) fork since you can do tasks usually associated with it, such as underplanting, with the trowel instead.

HOES The tools discussed so far are for digging in one form or another but you also need a couple of cultivators. A weeding hoe is top of my list because it will save you pounds in chemical weedkillers and a great deal of time crawling on your hands and knees trying to pull out all of your

DECEMBER

weeds one by one. But do be sure that you buy a push hoe, not a draw hoe. A push hoe – of which a Dutch hoe is the most familiar example works as its name implies by being pushed along the top of the soil in dry weather in order to sever weed seedlings and leave them to shrivel on the surface. A draw hoe is a quite different appliance used to pull soil towards you and has little use apart from earthing up potatoes, a task that can be done adequately enough with a spade.

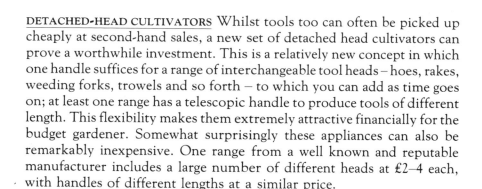

RAKES My second essential cultivator is a rake. As you look around the gardening world, you will soon realize that there are basically two types: one has a rigid head with about 10–12 short, stiff tines; the other has a much larger head with a mass of springy tines and is variously known as a spring tine, lawn or leaf rake. The budget gardener should choose the latter for it is much more versatile and so better value for money, being useful not only for lawn raking and leaf collecting but also for seed-bed preparation and other soil raking tasks.

DETACHED-HEAD CULTIVATORS Whilst tools too can often be picked up cheaply at second-hand sales, a new set of detached head cultivators can prove a worthwhile investment. This is a relatively new concept in which one handle suffices for a range of interchangeable tool heads – hoes, rakes, weeding forks, trowels and so forth – to which you can add as time goes on; at least one range has a telescopic handle to produce tools of different length. This flexibility makes them extremely attractive financially for the budget gardener. Somewhat surprisingly these appliances can also be remarkably inexpensive. One range from a well known and reputable manufacturer includes a large number of different heads at £2–4 each, with handles of different lengths at a similar price.

❀ **'BUDGET TIP'** A great many very inexpensive and often unbranded garden tools are likely to prove disastrous investments: you only need to use them once to discover why they are so cheap. It is far more cost-effective to choose those with a recognizable brand name.

CUTTING TOOLS In addition to the tools that actually make contact with soil, the budget gardener will need at least a couple of cutting tools:

DECEMBER

secateurs (or pruners as they are often called) and shears. You may prefer single bladed pruners (sometimes called anvil pattern) as these tend to be more robust and better able to cope with hard, woody stems. They are also better as second-hand buys for the single blade is much less likely to have been bent.

If, when buying shears, you can only afford one pair, do buy short-handled hedge shears. With a little back-bending you can manage to do the lawn edges with them and also use them for trimming back such plants as lavender and heather. If your only shears are long-handled lawn shears, you will find they are useless for any other task.

I have to say that there are few things in gardening more frustrating than a cutting tool that doesn't cut, either because it is too blunt or, worse, because its blades have been bent out of true. Second-hand cutters with the former defect can be put right by taking them to a reputable hardware store with a sharpening service; the chances are that those with the latter defect can't.

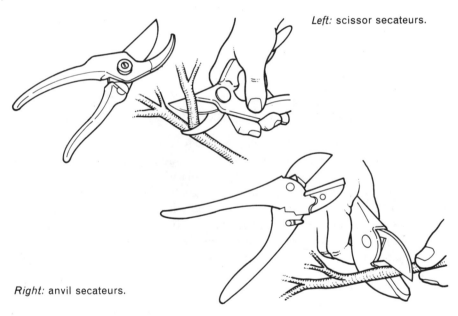

Left: scissor secateurs.

Right: anvil secateurs.

❀ **'BUDGET TIP'** When buying old, two-bladed scissor-secateurs or shears, do be sure that the blades slice neatly together, with no light visible between them.

CHRISTMAS AND THE GARDEN

I don't think many people would argue that Christmas has become a very expensive time of the year. On the one hand, it is also a time when gardening activities are at a fairly low ebb and so will not cause too much drain on the pocket while, on the other, the garden itself can actually contribute in a money-saving way towards the festivities, especially if you have stored and frozen vegetables and fruit to help spin out the menus. Although, as I've said before, few of us will be anything like self-sufficient from the kitchen garden this needn't matter. If you are only able to provide a few touches – the home-made apple sauce, the compote of home-grown and frozen fruit, the stuffing enhanced with home-produced herbs – these will save you a little extra expense and certainly be greatly appreciated by family and friends.

And what about gifts from the garden? Plants are always appreciated and yet pot plants seem to double in price at this time of year. If you have a greenhouse or even a decent-sized window-sill and are prepared to do a little planning in spring, one packet of seeds of the lovely foliage plant coleus could by now – at extremely low cost – have produced enough plants to give as presents to all of your friends – and still leave you plenty for yourself. And as there is so much variety in a packet of coleus, you can be pretty certain that no two people will have identical plants. There are naturally other pot plant possibilities too, but coleus combines cheapness with ease of cultivation.

CHRISTMAS DECORATIONS Christmas of course has much to do with decoration and so my first bit of advice concerns the Christmas tree itself. Provided you have a garden, there is absolutely no reason why you shouldn't re-use your tree from year to year. You must first buy one with good roots and then pot it into a plastic pot with either very good garden soil or, preferably, potting compost. Don't neglect the tree during the festivities – be sure that the pot stands in a saucer and that the compost is kept moist. If at all possible try to avoid positioning it very close to a radiator or other heater.

Once Christmas is over set it first in a fairly cool, but well lit, place and gradually, after another week or so, re-accustom it to life in the great outdoors. As soon as weather conditions allow, place it in a fairly sunny spot – but still in its pot, which should be sunk to the rim. During the summer, be sure that the tree is watered and given liquid fertilizer. With a reasonable slice of luck it should be ready for lifting again next December.

Among the trees that I have recommended for the small, budget garden (see p. 97) is the yellow-berried holly. If you have a reasonably well grown specimen of either yellow- or red-berried varieties, you can avoid having to buy holly by simply throwing some netting (an old net curtain will suffice) over a branch around the beginning of December. This will ensure that even in hard weather, the birds leave a few berries alone for

DECEMBER

you to cut off and enjoy. And it doesn't take me to tell you that with a little ingenuity, some oasis and a few pieces of chicken wire you can make use of all manner of garden oddments in the shape of evergreen foliage, nuts, conifer cones, even dried fungal bracket growths to good and decorative effect.

FESTIVE POT PLANTS The two most popular pot plants at Christmas are poinsettias and hyacinths – and far too many examples of both are wastefully thrown away when the New Year comes. As soon as the flowers fade on pot hyacinths cut off the dead flower stalks and apply some liquid fertilizer to the plants until the leaves eventually yellow and shrivel. Then they should be allowed to dry off, the bulbs lifted and stored ready for planting in the garden in autumn. Such hyacinths will never be quite as large and luxuriant as they were indoors and they certainly won't flower as early as Christmas but they will nonetheless add very usefully to the garden display at absolutely no cost.

My advice with poinsettias is, first, not to throw them away and, second, not to waste time, effort and money trying to induce them to produce red bracts again – it's very tricky to do satisfactorily. I suggest that you do as I do and treat your poinsettia exactly like any other green foliage plant. At no cost at all to you it will produce beautiful, lime-green leaves right through the year and makes a charming addition to any house plant display.

P lants for Christmas: coleus and (far right) poinsettia.

JOBS FOR DECEMBER

GENERAL

Clean and sharpen garden tools. They are a big and valuable investment and the better you take care of them, the longer they will last.

Try to knock off snow from trees and shrubs, especially from evergreens, as promptly as possible before its weight causes damage to branches.

Enjoy Christmas, look back with pleasure and pride on your achievements this year, and look forward to doing even better next season.

THE INDOOR GARDEN

If you buy indoor plants for Christmas save money by choosing those that can be re-used. Hyacinths and many types of primula are good bets as they can be planted in the garden afterwards. Avoid paper-white narcissi, which are useless once flowering is over.

For the period of the festivities, protect your permanent house plants by moving them into a cooler room where their chances of survival will be greatly enhanced – after all, our homes are probably heated to higher temperatures at Christmas than at any other time.

CONTAINERS

The relative inactivity of winter enables you to make good any damage to containers that has arisen during the summer. Home-made pots can be repainted while terracotta ones can be repaired very cost-effectively with a tube of epoxy resin.

❋ **'BUDGET TIP'** Never throw away broken or cracked terracotta pots. They repair very inexpensively and satisfactorily and, when plants are tumbling over the sides in the summer, no one will notice. But if a pot is totally smashed keep the pieces to use as 'crocks' to partially cover drainage holes in pot bases.

GREENHOUSES, COLD FRAMES AND CLOCHES

Be doubly sure that all is ready for the start of seed sowing in the coming weeks. Are all pots, seed trays and other containers clean and neatly stacked?

❋ **'BUDGET TIP'** Save money by re-using old plastic labels after cleaning them with a cloth and kitchen scouring powder.

A neat, tidy greenhouse and cold frame will positively invite you to make a start as soon as temperatures rise.

LAWN

Keep off the lawn as much as possible in December, especially when it is frozen. Only in very mild spells can you continue with raking and general tidying up.

In very mild years the grass will continue to grow and so mowing can continue – I mowed my lawn on New Year's Eve a few years ago.

THE FLOWER GARDEN

This is the best time for raising alpine plants by the cheapest way possible

DECEMBER

DECEMBER

– from seed – as they require the frost and cold of the winter to help them to germinate. Sow them now in a soil-based, gritty compost in shallow pots and leave them outside until the spring.

Any winter-flowering plants in the garden – particularly rock garden plants – that have buds will produce a better show of flowers if they are given a little protection. A simple cloche (see p. 18) will do the trick.

VEGETABLES

If you are growing carrots, they can safely be stored in the soil much more reliably than digging them up. But it will help to cut off the tops at the beginning of December and preferably put some straw over them, anchored in place with a few spadesful of soil.

Any vegetables that you intend to dig from the garden for use at Christmas should be dug when the weather is mild and a few days in advance.

Digging should be completed by December as the soil is likely to become much less easily workable once the New Year turns.

FRUIT

Continue to check stored apples and pears as in November.

Check over strawberry plants and snip off browned and yellowed foliage.

At the end of December, provided the weather is mild, make a start on spraying fruit bushes and trees with tar oil to control insect pests.

TREES AND SHRUBS

Continue to check for hollows at the base of staked trees and ensure that they are secure. Even modest winter gales can cause movement and weakening of supports.

CLIMBERS

Wisterias should have their second pruning of the year this month. The shoots that were cut back in July should now be cut back further, to about 5 cm (2 in) from the base.

❀ **'BUDGET TIP'** While pruning wisteria do take the opportunity to pull away any shoots that threaten to penetrate beneath tiles, before they do costly damage.

Check that trellises and other structures used to support climbers are sound. You have an ideal opportunity to work on them now that deciduous climbers are leafless.